CW01659076

SNAPREVISE

SnapRevise Text Guide: Mrs Dalloway by Virginia Woolf

Jayden Rothwell

InStudent Education UK Ltd owner of SnapRevise® trademark.
43 Priston Close, Worle, BS22 7FL, Weston-Super-Mare, United Kingdom

www.snaprevise.co.uk

Title: Mrs Dalloway by Virginia Woolf
ISBN: 978-1-917424-29-5

Published by InStudent Education UK Ltd CN 15550989 under licence from InStudent Publishing Pty Ltd.
ACN 624 188101

Preface

Mrs Dalloway is a truly wonderful text. Its style is engaging and likely to be very different to texts you usually study. *Mrs Dalloway* is all about humanity. It explores the way we think, interact with society, and pursue our dreams.

This is a tricky novel to read because of the way it seamlessly shifts between the past and present, along with presenting multiple points of view. The style is extremely intimate and written so that you develop connections and understandings of the inner workings of each character. This makes it an enjoyable read once you get past the initial headache!

This is a novel that leaves you with burning questions and lots to consider. So, I encourage you to read it thoroughly and make your own interpretations as you go. This Text Guide analyses the major themes, contextual influences, characters, quotes, and structural features as a resource for you, but you will always find it easier to write about your own ideas. Using multiple resources is always a great way of exposing yourself to different perspectives.

— Jayden Rothwell

Contents

Chapter 1

Nutshell Summary

Woolf's writing is quite complex and difficult to read. Some sections may need to be read a few times to properly understand what is being said or described. This difficulty is to do with Woolf's style – as a prominent Modernist author, Woolf experimented with narrative structure and form. This includes flashbacks a stream of consciousness style where we delve into the minds of each character. Woolf also transitions seamlessly between the past and present and consistently shifts perspectives to further complicate the novel.

The complexity of Woolf's style often results in multiple viable interpretations of meaning. It can also have the unintended effect of undermining the actual message intended by Woolf. Though we cannot know for sure, it's possible Woolf wrote in this way because her novel may have alienated readers in her 1925 context if she was too direct with her messages. This is because the society of the time was less receptive to criticisms of conventions and traditions. Therefore, to make sure her work was not silenced, Woolf may have employed this style to keep the true meaning hidden beneath layers of meaning that need to be uncovered.

As you read Virginia Woolf's *Mrs Dalloway*, you are transported into the minds of Woolf's characters. You witness the destabilisation of post-war London and the psychological trauma that has infected society. You come to understand the misery and suffering of the characters who are united in their inability to fulfil their dreams. *Mrs Dalloway* represents the drudgery of adulthood and the never-ending battle for happiness and connection.

The main character, Clarissa Dalloway, is in her fifties. She is realising that she is not satisfied with her life as insecurity bubbles to the surface of her well-constructed exterior. She wants to be admired and seen as a member of high society, but this is not enough to make her happy. Like most people, Clarissa can only find true happiness if she forgets about the judgement of others and pursues her passions freely. This requires change, taking risks, and being bold.

Mrs Dalloway is a story seemingly with no plot, no tangible development, and no clear resolution. Rather, it focuses on a fairly ordinary day where we see fairly ordinary people navigating life's challenges. This focus on the uninteresting, uninspiring moments of life capture a reality that faces us all; that is, the struggle to achieve our aspirations. The novel is driven by the glimpses we get into the worlds of each character. We see their struggles, flaws, and hopes. It is a reflection of our own existence as we navigate the uncertainty and turmoil of society whilst battling insecurity, fear, and disappointment.

Chapter 2

Background Information

Mrs Dalloway was published in 1925. At that time, there was a notable cultural shift as a result of the catastrophic First World War and the retreat from traditional Victorian values. Woolf's novel was shaped greatly by her life experiences and the way she perceived the world and its institutions. Woolf had suffered from mental illness throughout her life, consistently causing her distress and pain. This interfered with her passion of writing and made her more critical of traditional structures of society that she believed had failed her and others. Despite being written in the early 20th century, Woolf's novel is still relevant to modern readers through the questions it raises on the value and purpose of life.

The life of Virginia Woolf

Virginia Woolf was born in 1882 in London, to a wealthy family well-connected to literature. Her interest in literature stemmed from her father, Leslie Stephen, and she used his library to educate herself at home. Her mother, Julia Jackson, died in 1895, which caused Woolf's first mental breakdown at age 13. Her half-sister, Stella Duckworth, died two years later, leading to Woolf's second mental breakdown. She continued to suffer from mental instability throughout her life, with her breakdowns characterised by insomnia, headaches, irritability, and nervousness.

Woolf's father died in 1904, after which Woolf started publishing her first essays. Woolf felt restricted by her father, admitting that if her father had not died, he would have inhibited her creativity and she never would have written her essays and novels. In 1912, Virginia Woolf married Leonard Woolf and took his surname through marriage. He was a close friend that she bonded with over their intellectual curiosity and **contempt** for traditional structures. With Leonard, Woolf felt liberated from a society she viewed as repressive.

Throughout her life, Woolf had written many novels and essays. Woolf's first novel, *The Voyage Out*, was published in 1915. After finishing this novel, Woolf developed excruciating headaches and insomnia. She had been briefly institutionalised multiple times, although her condition never truly went away. Woolf continued to experience periods of depression and **psychosis**. She was never truly at peace, although she found great comfort in her literary works, something she viewed as a way of dealing with her illness.

Contempt: to have disrespect or disdain for something.

Psychosis: a sense of disconnection from reality which can cause delusions.

Woolf made some attempts to seek help from doctors, however, they were often dismissive of her and failed to address her illness due to a lack of understanding of mental illnesses at the time, particularly in women. Doctors had advised her that she simply needed some rest and relaxation. As Woolf's problems continued to reappear throughout her life, she was diagnosed with lung trouble and heart trouble. Again, the advice was to merely rest and relax. It is believed by psychiatrists today that Woolf suffered from **bipolar disorder** which consistently resurfaced throughout her life.

In 1940, Woolf's insomnia and nervousness had returned. The escalation of World War II and the loss of her London home from German bombing contributed to her anxiety and **disarray**. Woolf feared that she was going insane and no longer had the strength and the will to battle her delusions once more. She drowned herself in a river in March 1941 at the age of 59. Woolf had previously attempted suicide at least once by overdosing on tablets.

There are some notable parallels between Woolf's life and the life of Clarissa Dalloway. However, it is important to recognise that Clarissa is a distinct character, separate from the author, and should not be seen **reductively** as an extension of Woolf's identity.

Cultural changes

The 1800s saw huge technological advancements and industrialisation, particularly in machinery and textiles. This led to increased economic prosperity and the development of the middle class, which is broadly defined as the group of people with a comfortable socioeconomic status. Workers' rights were strengthened due to the influence of expanding **trade unions** which had spread across Britain. The spread of democracy increased the power of the rapidly growing middle class and eroded old systems where **aristocrats** controlled the government.

Aftermath of the First World War

The First World War (fought mostly in Europe from July 1914 to November 1918) left British society with an overwhelming sense of loss and despair. Hundreds of thousands of British men were killed during the conflict, and the United Kingdom was devastated economically. The incredible loss and trauma of the war permeated British society, leading to great **disillusionment** with traditional class systems and social structures. The ruins of the war transformed British society, causing a rejection of conservative principles, which led to social reform, the growth of the Labour Party, and the partial right to vote for women. The membership of trade unions had also risen substantially during the war from 4.1 million in 1914 to 6.5 million in 1918.

Bipolar disorder: a mental disorder that causes extreme shifts in mood, typically depressive lows and energised highs.

Disarray: a state of disorganisation or chaos.

Reductive: something oversimplified or crude that ignores details.

Trade unions: organisations of workers who can collectively negotiate for better pay and conditions on behalf of all workers.

Aristocrats: the upper class elites of a society who hold vast wealth and influence.

Disillusion: disappointment from realising that something is not as good as it once seemed.

Tumultuous: unstable, disorderly, and confusing.

Zeitgeist: the 'spirit of the time,' or what it feels like to be living in society at a certain point of history.

Apathy: having no emotions or empathy.

PTSD: the inability to recover from traumatic experiences which can cause nightmares, anxiety, or depression.

Archetype: the typical associations of a character or idea.

The British empire had been declining in its influence and power in the aftermath of the war. Independence movements led to Britain losing territory across the world. In 1922 alone, both Ireland and Egypt achieved independence from the United Kingdom. Many British colonies fought for and succeeded in attaining independence over the following years.

The **tumultuous** time immediately after the war was captured by Woolf who presents characters alienated from society and incapable of finding a sense of purpose. The stream of consciousness style used by Woolf reflects this disjointed **zeitgeist** and emphasising the uncertainty of the period. Woolf sought to critique and expose the **apathy** of British society that had ignored the effects of the war and stifled emotions and sensitivities.

Mental illness

The conditions soldiers experienced throughout the war were harsh, relentless, and traumatic. Soldiers witnessed horrific deaths, crippling injuries, and disease, leaving them psychologically scarred. This caused many soldiers to detach from reality, often having experiencing anxiety, nightmares, and a difficulty sleeping and engaging with others. A common war injury was 'shell shock,' and its effects extended beyond the war, with symptoms often persisting for the rest of one's life. This made it extremely difficult for returning soldiers to re-enter normal society and employment.

Mental illness was poorly understood at the time, and 'shell shock' is better understood in contemporary society as post-traumatic stress disorder **(PTSD)**. This conflicted with the **archetype** of soldiers as strong and heroic. Therefore, having PTSD was at the time viewed as a personal weakness or a failure of character. As a result, treatments were brutal and sought to 'snap' a veteran out of cowardice rather than address their profound psychological trauma. Some treatments involved electroshock therapy, causing many veterans to instead resort to self-medication or other destructive coping mechanisms like drugs and alcohol.

Woolf's own experiences with mental illness and the lack of acceptance within society and medical institutions influence the depiction of the character Septimus Warren Smith. Septimus, a World War I veteran, was a victim of the war and suffers from PTSD, but was dismissed by doctors as merely weak, leaving him dejected and isolated. Septimus echoes Woolf's experiences and fragile state of mind; they both had visions of birds talking in Greek and attempted suicide by jumping out of a window.

Feminism

The Victorian era (the period of Queen Victoria's reign from 1837 to 1901) was a time of rigid expectations and gender roles for women. Their primary responsibility was seen to be in domestic life, particularly caring for their husbands and children. Women were largely excluded from the public sphere and were pressured to maintain an outward appearance of purity and passivity. The **patriarchal** society of the time meant that Woolf was unable to attend university like her brothers, leaving her resentful.

Patriarchal: a society controlled by and structured around men.

The early 20th century saw the beginning of a shift from these Victorian ideals, with many women becoming more active in society. This led to a loosening of the strict societal expectations of women, enabling greater opportunities and independence.

Women **suffragettes** passionately campaigned for the right to vote in the early 1900s. Suffragettes protested and went on hunger strikes to raise awareness for their cause and expose the institutional sexism they faced and their discrimination from the public sphere. In 1918, women over the age of 30 were granted the right to vote if they met some property qualifications. This enabled around 8.4 million women to vote. It was not until 1928 that all women over the age of 21 were able to vote in Britain and hence had the same voting eligibility as men.

Suffragettes: people who fought for women's right to vote.

World War I saw one third of the men in the United Kingdom labour force moved to military service. This increased the demand for industrial labour, especially in munitions factories. Many women were able to temporarily fill these positions on the home front, elevating them to a more active role within society. Upon the end of the war, some employed women were obliged to forfeit their jobs to returning soldiers. Women's sacrifices and contribution to the war effort advanced the feminist cause and was appreciated by British society.

Despite the social shift and progress made, women were still largely excluded from the public domain. Woolf partially attributed her mental condition to the repressive nature of society. Woolf explores the complexity of female characters and their individual motivations, giving a voice and depth to characters that feel constricted by society.

Chapter 3

Section-by-Section Analysis

KEY POINT :
Mrs Dalloway contains **no chapters** and takes place over a single day. It constantly shifts perspectives with the use of stream of consciousness to express each character's thoughts.

To make it easier to follow the summary and analysis, this Text Guide will divide the novel into 12 sections, but these sections **should not** be referred to when discussing the text or writing an essay!

Furthermore, since there is very little plot and few major events in this text, this part will focus mainly on analysis. Lots of quotes from the text are included and analysed, but keep in mind that you are encouraged to draw your own interpretations.

Section 1

The novel begins uneventfully on an ordinary day in mid June 1923 from the perspective of Clarissa Dalloway, a 51 year old member of London's high society. She is concerned greatly with her reputation and status. Clarissa had suffered from influenza which has given her heart trouble. She is throwing a party at night and her housekeeper, Lucy, is busy getting everything ready. The opening line is Clarissa's assertive declaration that she will go and buy the flowers for the party "herself." This sets the stage for the novel's examination of autonomy and self-reflection. However, the title itself, *Mrs Dalloway*, places emphasis on her title rather than her name, Clarissa. The patriarchal society meant women were often seen as an extension of their husband. This attaches Clarissa to her husband, Richard Dalloway – a conservative politician – distancing Clarissa from her identity. It furthers the idea that the 'Clarissa' that had existed as a youth has now decayed, and she has now emerged as Mrs Dalloway, a respectable member of the upper class.

Vitality: energy and strength, full of life force.

Ominous: foreboding or foreshadowing something bad that is yet to come.

Clarissa enjoys the fresh early morning air which is "like the flap of a wave; the kiss of a wave; chill and sharp." The air is a source of **vitality** for her, filling her with energy and confidence. Yet she would always get an uneasy feeling that something bad was coming, even when she was eighteen at Bourton (a costal English town). This **ominous** mood is furthered through the image of smoke, suggesting some sort of disturbance. Clarissa remembers that Peter Walsh, her old friend from Bourton, is expected to return from India soon. Whilst in India, Peter had married a woman called Daisy, though Clarissa does not know this. The memory of Peter immediately after Clarissa's apprehensive feeling foreshadows that Peter's return is the disturbance.

Clarissa enjoys the bustling city and is enthralled by "the uproar; the carriages, motor cars, omnibuses, vans, sandwich men shuffling and swinging." This description of a lively, loud city is **juxtaposed** with "the silence; the mist; the hum; the slow-swimming happy ducks; the pouched birds waddling" as she enters the natural world of the park. Clarissa runs into Hugh Whitbread, another old friend from Bourton, who says he will be attending her party with his wife, Evelyn. Evelyn was often sick, and Clarissa enjoyed making visits to her as she was always "pleased as she came in." From this, we can infer that Clarissa finds great joy in being respected and included by others.

Juxtapose: to place two things next to each other to create a contrast.

The calmer, quieter park encourages Clarissa to reflect on her life. She reminisces about Peter as she is excited for his upcoming return. She recalls that he could be "intolerable" and "impossible," but also "adorable." They had a confusing relationship given their past; Peter had described Clarissa's desire to please and be loved by all as "the perfect hostess," which bothered Clarissa as a critique of her shallowness and **vanity.**

Vanity: pride in oneself or one's appearance.

Clarissa leads a meticulous and organised life as "she sliced like a knife through everything; at the same time was outside, looking on." This metaphor represents how she lacks emotion and sincerity in her actions, reflecting how she feels isolated like an observer rather than an active participant. This is ironic as Clarissa is the central character, yet she lacks the substance to be noteworthy beyond her exterior. This emphasises her lack of identity and the "perpetual sense, as she watched the taxi cabs, of being out, out, far out to sea and alone." The taxi cabs symbolise movement and progression, yet Clarissa can only "watch" them from afar as she is not undertaking such a journey; she remains stationary and empty.

Clarissa paradoxically "felt very young; at the same time unspeakably aged," which accentuates Clarissa's struggle to make sense of and reconcile her youthful ambitions with the **mundanity** of her present life. She is intrigued by the finality of death and wondered if the prospect of death should evoke resentment or consolation. The questioning "did it matter that she must inevitably cease completely" forces Clarissa to reflect on the worth of her life and what she has become.

Mundanity: boring, monotonous, everyday concerns.

The war had ended five years ago, but its effects have persisted. People are still suffering from the loss of soldiers and had caused in "all men and women, a well of tears." The turbulence of the war has instilled an overwhelming sense of uncertainty within the British population. The social and economic impacts and the increasing independence of British colonies has challenged traditional structures and undermined Britain's perception of **infallibility**.

Infallibility: inability to have flaws, make mistakes, or be wrong about something.

The **status quo** is seen as repressive and is emblematic of Clarissa's trapped self. She lacks control and autonomy as she has given in to society's expectations of her as a member of high society. This is symbolised as the "policeman held up his hand" to prevent her from crossing the street.

Status quo: the traditional way things are done; the accepted norms in society.

Lament: to express sorrow or regret.

Even the most mundane acts are limited, highlighting the extent to which she is stifled by society. Clarissa walks down Bond Street and **laments** her position in life: "oh if she could have had her life over again!" Clarissa is desperate to find happiness and to no longer be gripped by regret. Yet there is no way for her to change the past; she is forced to deal with her present body which "seemed nothing – nothing at all." The repetition of "nothing" suggests that her character is defined only by what exists around her. The image of the bustling city as a source of life reflects the lack of inner substance that is pivotal for Clarissa's fulfilment.

Relegate: to limit or assign a lower rank to someone.

She feels invisible, with "there being no more marrying, no more having of children now, but only this astonishing and rather solemn progress." Since the patriarchal society at the time largely excluded women from the public sphere, **relegating** them to domestic duties of marriage and motherhood, marriage and having children were seen to be key to happiness and a sense of purpose. However, Clarissa is well past that phase, being in her fifties now with her daughter approaching adulthood. Thus, Clarissa feels that she does not exist beyond her obligations of womanhood.

Clarissa's 17 year old daughter, Elizabeth Dalloway, has turned religious as a result of the influence of Doris Kilman who tutors Elizabeth in history. Miss Kilman and Clarissa despise each other and the influence they each have on Elizabeth. Clarissa feels alienated from Elizabeth as she is changing and embracing religion. Clarissa finds Miss Kilman unpleasant and spiteful as "you feel her superiority, your inferiority; how poor she was; how rich you were... poor embittered unfortunate creature!" Clarissa's sarcastic tone shows her distaste for those she viewed as beneath her, reflecting Clarissa's obsession with class and reputation.

Disdain: feeling that someone is unworthy of one's respect.

Clarissa's hatred and **disdain** for Miss Kilman "rasped her, though, to have stirring about in her this brutal monster!" The connotation of "rasped" and "brutal monster" emphasises the debilitating nature of Clarissa's illness and how it disturbs her. Her illness makes Clarissa bitter and hostile, constantly resurfacing as "the brute would be stirring, this hatred." The dehumanisation of Clarissa's illness through "brute" attempts to separate Clarissa's hatred and bitterness from her personality.

When Clarissa arrives at the florist, her hatred softens for the moment as she is fascinated by the flowers. Miss Pym, who works in the store, liked Clarissa, which fills Clarissa with joy, "a wave which she let flow over her and surmount that hatred, that monster, surmount it all," revealing how human connection can overcome such self-destructive hatred. It offers some hope for Clarissa and puts her at peace, though this moment is fleeting as Clarissa is quickly interrupted by the sound of a pistol firing outside. The jarring sound and image of a pistol undercuts the joy she felt. This moment ends as they discover that the sound is not actually a pistol, but a motor car instead.

Section 2

The novel resumes outside the shop where Clarissa is buying flowers, with the startling sound of the motor having attracted the attention of a crowd. As the crowd realises that the sound was not of a pistol, their faces fall from panic to "sudden sobriety and stillness upon faces which a second before had been utterly disorderly." The disarray is then tamed by "the voice of authority" that announced confidently that the car was the Prime Minister's car.

The perspective now shifts to Septimus Warren Smith, who also heard the announcement of the Prime Minister's car. Septimus is about thirty years old and had served honourably in the war. He is described as "pale-faced, beak-nosed, wearing brown shoes and a shabby overcoat," all fairly ordinary characteristics and garments with nothing too special or noteworthy about him. This is intentional as his experiences are common for many returning soldiers attempting to reintegrate into British society and establish a sense of normality. Septimus is filled with anxiety and his eyes "had that look of **apprehension** in them which makes complete strangers apprehensive too." The perceived infectious nature of his apprehension emphasises his incredible suffering that paralyses him. Much like Clarissa, Septimus is plagued by uncertainty and fear.

Apprehension: anxiety and uneasiness.

Septimus is startled by the sound and questions "the world has raised its whip; where will it descend?" The rhetorical question reflects the powerlessness of Septimus and others to the oppressive society that has abandoned him. It foreshadows that the world will cause **indiscriminate** pain and suffering with no chance to escape its wrath. Septimus, having served in the war and witnessed death and destruction, suffers from PTSD.

Indiscriminate: non-selective, affecting all people.

The loud sound of the car likely triggered memories of battle, causing fear as "the world wavered and quivered and threatened to burst into flames." This visual imagery represents the intensity of his fear and his **volatile** state of mind, ready to ignite; the way Septimus is afraid of the sound of a car reflects the extent of his trauma. His wife, Lucrezia Warren Smith, begs Septimus to continue walking. Lucrezia is aged 24 and met Septimus after the war in Italy and promptly married and moved to London with him. It is mentioned that Septimus has spoken of a desire to kill himself in the past.

Volatile: unpredictable and changing rapidly.

The crowd is fascinated by the car and there is much speculation of who was inside. Clarissa thinks it could be the Queen, but whoever it is, "greatness was seated within; greatness was passing, hidden." The repetition highlights the symbolic nature of royalty and the power it represents. The crowd is attached more to this symbol than to the person within the car, which is currently blocked by an omnibus.

There are many vehicles around which contain "British middle classes sitting sideways on the tops of omnibuses with parcels and umbrellas." This expresses the growing power of the middle class. They are positioned above the Prime Minister's car and as an obstacle, symbolising the changing power dynamics within British society.

Clarissa finds it ironic that "the Queen herself held up; the Queen herself unable to pass" as an allusion to the decline of the British Empire despite its appearance of infallibility. The impacts of the war have furthered this decline, especially through the independence of many British colonies. The middle class is ever-growing and threatens the traditional structure of society that have enabled the elites to thrive unchecked. The middle class is becoming a formidable new social strata of society that wield great political power. As the omnibus makes way for the car, it passes "slowly and very silently," further reflecting the decay of the British Empire that is now beholden to the middle class.

This sense of social and political upheaval in the post-war period is described as a "ripple" and a "vibration" that no "mathematical instrument" is capable of detecting. This reveals that the most significant change is within society itself; the way people feel about their political system and leaders. The system that has persisted appears largely inadequate in serving the common people and the impression is given that the aristocrats had abandoned the lower class and escaped the suffering and loss of the war. The way everyone momentarily stopped what they were doing and stared at the car as it was blocked represents the widespread disillusionment as "strangers looked at each other and thought of the dead; of the flag; of Empire."

The Prime Minister's car turns down another street and can no longer be seen. Clarissa notices a group of "tall men, men of robust physique, well-dressed men" and thinks it is strange the way they seem unaffected by the vibration that had unnerved the crowd. The men are depicted as strong and defenders of tradition. This sense of loyalty is criticised by Woolf as undeserving and against their own interests. As the men stand straighter, signifying their confidence, they "seemed ready to attend their Sovereign, if need be, to the cannon's mouth, as their ancestors had done before them." The symbolism of the cannon's mouth expresses their relationship to power and tradition. Their loyalty and servitude are a resource to the aristocracy, with their **compliance** allowing the elites to remain in control and avoid responsibility and consequences. It suggests the **inevitability** that the men will be consumed by the oppressive society that they willingly protect. The reference to ancestors before them doing the same shows the perpetual cycle that Woolf despises. This cycle is the ruling class maintaining power at the expense of the lower classes, suggesting that some drastic change needs to occur to ascertain true equality and freedom within society.

Compliance: obedience to a command or expectation.

Inevitable: something that is unavoidable.

At the same time, a separate crowd has gathered outside the gates of Buckingham Palace (the residence of the royal family). These people are impoverished and are desperate for some form of recognition. They "let rumour accumulate in their veins and thrill the nerves in their thighs at the thought of Royalty looking at them; the Queen bowing; the Prince saluting." More people arrive and attach themselves to the desire to be noticed. The crowd reflects the vast disconnection between the upper **echelon** of society that wields immense power and the poor that are victims and facing injustice. The gate itself is a metaphor for this barrier and reinforces the oppressive nature of the ruling class that subdues its citizens. The crowd's attachment to royalty reflects the desire of the poor to **transcend** their uninspiring and repressed lives.

Echelon: a level or rank in society.

Transcend: to move beyond boundaries.

Emily Coates, a part of the crowd outside Buckingham Palace, thinks about the magnitude of the Palace, pondering how many housemaids and bedrooms lie within. She then looks into the sky as the sound of an aeroplane approaches which "bored ominously into the ears of the crowd." The aural imagery highlights the brief terror in the crowd to the sound, reflecting the persisting trauma of the war as the sound reminds them of the aerial bombardments of London. It suggests that society has not moved on or finished grappling with the impacts of the war despite the dismissal and inaction of British government. The crowd's attention is shifted towards the sky as the plane leaves a trail of smoke as if writing letters.

The letters are too difficult to read as "only for a moment did they lie still; then they moved and melted and were rubbed out up in the sky". The **ephemeral** nature of the letters creates uncertainty about the message and its meaning, reflecting the disjointed world and the inability to find certainty and contentment. The crowd is entranced by the plane's movement as "the whole world became perfectly silent". The plane offers some hope of a greater purpose "in this extraordinary silence and peace, in this pallor, in this purity." For a brief moment, the crowd is at peace, experiencing the serenity they crave.

Ephemeral: lasting only for a short time; something transitory or fleeting.

The plane continues to write letters – which are still too difficult to make out – as the plane goes out of sight behind clouds. The clouds "moved freely, as if destined to cross from West to East on a mission of the greatest importance which would never be revealed". The juxtaposition of the clouds' seemingly essential mission that can't be understood or known reflects the hollowness of the crowd's hope. Ultimately, there are no answers and no escape from their suffering and their existence. Their attachment to royalty, then, is seen as nothing more than a way of coping with the injustice of their lives, but there is no substance in this hope.

We return to Septimus and Lucrezia, who are now in Regent's Park. Septimus is not well and is seeing things that aren't really there. Lucrezia attempts to distract Septimus by encouraging him to look up at the sky as the plane tried to write a message. Lucrezia was advised by Dr Holmes to keep Septimus distracted and to try get him interested in things besides himself. Septimus thinks the plane is writing a message directly to him and he is marvelled by "this beauty, this exquisite beauty, and tears filled his eyes as he looked at the smoke words languishing and melting." His extreme reaction to an ordinary plane represents the fragility of his mind and how he is susceptible to delusions. A nursemaid says that the plane is advertising toffee. There is no deeper message for Septimus, yet he sinks further into his delusional and irrational state.

Septimus' visions worsen as he now sees trees move and believes them to be living entities. The trees "beckoned; leaves were alive; trees were alive. And the leaves being connected by millions of fibres with his own body." The beckoning of trees reflects Septimus' descent into insanity as he loses sense of reality. Though this may be founded in the real world (i.e. the trees are in fact "alive"), his vulnerability is exemplified through his fixation on the imagery of millions of interconnected fibres, suggesting that he has lost his identity and is controlled by his visions.

Lucrezia is distraught by Septimus' state of mind. She attempts to call Septimus out of his trance-like state, then flees to the fountain. Lucrezia is tired of the way he rarely engages with her and constantly stares into nothing. She looks back at him sitting by himself with a shabby overcoat and is confused by how he ended up this way. She believes his talk of killing himself is pure cowardice, yet this confuses her as she acknowledges Septimus had fought bravely during the war. Moreover, Dr Holmes has said that Septimus is not ill (which is unsurprising to us as contemporary readers who know how poorly mental health conditions like PTSD were treated during this time), which confuses Lucrezia further.

Lucrezia concludes that Septimus must just be selfish. She is saddened by the way he no longer recognises her or compliments her, reflecting their strained relationship as a result of Septimus' illness. Lucrezia is suffering greatly due to his condition as she had moved to London for Septimus, leaving her isolated from her friends and family in Italy. She still very much loves Septimus but dealing with him is taxing on her. Lucrezia has become much thinner and her wedding ring no longer fits her finger – a symbol for the toll this has taken on her physical existence and the state of their relationship. Lucrezia feels lost and silenced as "dark descends, pours over the outlines of houses and towers; bleak hillsides soften and fall in." The imagery of darkness consuming houses and towers suggests that there is little hope or escape. Lucrezia is resigned to a lonely existence, with her youth and love "robbed of colour, blank of windows." This reflects the dull, insipid life she now lives and the emptiness of her soul.

Lucrezia cries at the fountain, declaring that she is alone and hopes that, "perhaps at midnight, when all boundaries are lost, the country reverts to its ancient shape, as the Romans saw it". This reflects the perception that society has become less free over time and that Septimus and Lucrezia are victims of a society that doesn't prioritise **autonomy** of individuals. There is a sense of longing for the "ancient shape" of liberation and personal control.

Autonomy: independence and the ability to control one's own life.

Lucrezia returns to Septimus who is now singing along with sparrows, believing that they are speaking to him in Greek. They tell him the secrets of the universe, that there is no death and no crime. Septimus then has a vision of Evans, who was Septimus' officer during the war and close friend before he was killed in battle. Lucrezia interrupts Septimus, annoying him as she again tried to draw his attention elsewhere to "real things." Septimus is trapped in the "that eternal suffering, that eternal loneliness" as he is detached from reality.

Maisie Johnson, a 19 year old woman who just arrived in London, asked Septimus and Lucrezia for directions and found them to be quite "**queer**." Simply being in the presence of them plunges Maisie Johnson into the same existential dread as she questions her decision to come to London. She "joined that gently trudging, vaguely gazing" plight of uncertainty that suppresses one's hope and happiness. It seems that all characters in *Mrs Dalloway* suffer from this dread, permeating society.

Queer: to act in a strange or odd way.

The plane is coming to the end of its message and symbolises the life of the characters within the story. There is great anticipation in the plane's message, reflecting the characters' ambitions and aspirations for meaning. Yet the plane ends with no excitement as "away and away the aeroplane shot, till it was nothing but a bright spark." This signifies the inevitability of one's mortality and that everyone will fade into obscurity at some point.

The suspense of the plane that "sped of its own free will. And now, curving up and up, straight up, like something mounting in ecstasy" is juxtaposed by its mundanity as it advertised toffee and "poured white smoke looping, writing a T, an O, an F." This scene ends with this bleak image of life, suggesting that most people lead mundane lives and never see their ambitions become a reality.

Section 3

We return to the perspective of Clarissa who is returning home with the flowers she bought. She is experiencing a moment of bliss as "moments like this are buds on the tree of life." Buds and trees symbolise growth, suggesting that Clarissa's joy may spread and allow her to find happiness. Instead, Clarissa's moments of joy are always short-lived, communicating the tragedy and suffering of Clarissa's life. Woolf intentionally exploits this tragedy to express the depths of Clarissa's despair, how it seems impossible for her to progress and **elude** her trauma.

Elude: to escape or avoid.

Clarissa finds a note on the telephone pad written by Lucy. It is an invitation for Richard to attend lunch with Lady Bruton, a member of the upper class. Clarissa's joy is undercut by the discovery that she had been excluded and not invited to lunch. She is filled with disappointment and Lucy takes her parasol, "handled it like a sacred weapon which a Goddess, having acquitted herself honourably in the field of battle, sheds." This metaphor emphasises Clarissa's suffering as she feels unworthy and ignored. Woolf uses images of war to suggest that the true battles of life are not in the context of war itself but the internal battle for control and acceptance.

Clarissa is envious of Lady Bruton's reputation for her "extraordinarily amusing" lunch parties. Clarissa repeats this phrase which shows how she desires the respectability and status of Lady Bruton. Clarissa remarks that Lady Bruton's face has aged significantly "as if it had been a dial cut in impassive stone, the dwindling of life; how year by year her share was sliced." The implication is that death is inevitable and that old age is restrictive of one's dreams. Clarissa has aged as well, now in her fifties. She is not yet truly fulfilled and her soul is gradually **eroding** and she must come to terms with "the dwindling of life."

Eroding: being worn away or gradually destroyed over time.

Clarissa retreats slowly upstairs and goes to her bedroom. She feels trapped and is unable to be at peace with her illness as symbolised through the diminishing size of her bed – "narrower and narrower would her bed be." Beds represent rest, comfort and peace, yet Clarissa's is metaphorically narrowing which reflects her immense internal suffering that she can not escape. Even in the privacy of her bedroom, completely alone, she is still plagued by this sense of inadequacy despite the contented exterior she presents.

Clarissa has experienced love for women in the past. As she has given in to these feelings, she has been overcome by the "pressure of **rapture**, which split its thin skin and gushed and poured with an extraordinary alleviation over the cracks and sores!" The religious allusion of rapture emphasises the magnitude of Clarissa's love for women, how liberating it is that it overpowers cracks and sores of self-doubt. Clarissa had been in a relationship with Sally Seton in the old days at Bourton.

Rapture: a Christian belief in the end of the world where believers would ascend to heaven.

Sally Seton was adventurous and challenged traditional ideas. Clarissa thinks back to when they first met at Bourton and how Sally "made her feel, for the first time, how sheltered the life at Bourton was." After her mother and sister died, she was raised mostly by Aunt Helena who never quite liked discussion of anything, so as an outsider, Clarissa was intrigued by Sally and her teachings. They discussed sex, how to reform the world and how to create a freer society where private property is abolished. These newer, more radical ideas **catalysed** Clarissa's passion for reading.

Catalysed: to spark or cause something to begin.

Clarissa and Sally spoke about marriage constantly but always viewed it as a "catastrophe," which is a highly subversive idea for a time period in which marriage **reified** the oppressive norms and institutions whereby men wielded all the power. Clarissa and Sally's rejection of marriage reflects their desire to **usurp** societal boundaries and find emotional satisfaction. Their relationship and love are a sort of covert rebellion.

Reified: to reinforce something abstract in the form of something real.

Usurp: to seize or take control of something.

Clarissa admired the way Sally seemed totally free and uncaring of social or gender expectations as "the charm was overpowering." She was reckless, untidy and did not care much if people saw her naked. Clarissa laments that these moments of hope and freedom are absent in her present state as "she could not even get an echo of her old emotion." She attempts to revive that old feeling of ecstasy and liberation by doing her hair the same way she did back in Bourton. She thought of how she was always so excited to see Sally and professed "if it were now to die 'twere now to be most happy." This is an intertextual allusion to *Othello* that reflects the power of love as a way of finding happiness (this line is said by the character Othello when he reunites with Desdemona, the woman he loves).

Clarissa thinks back to a night where she had dinner with Sally. Sally appeared to be "glowing, like some bird or air ball that has flown in." This represents the Sally's vibrancy as she seems to be completely free like a bird. Sally is seen as an outsider, living and acting beyond society. Sally had kissed Clarissa that night which Clarissa felt was a gift, "a diamond, something infinitely precious." Despite Clarissa's current longing for reputation and status, she still has fondness for her youth with Sally. This positions the reader to see love and human connection as integral to happiness.

Peter had interrupted them and Clarissa thought he was jealous and wanted to disrupt their companionship and deep bond. Clarissa wonders if Peter will think she has aged when he returns as "since her illness she had turned almost white." Clarissa is determined to give an amazing party to honour herself. She hopes that people do not see what lies within her, the "other sides of her – faults, jealousies, vanities, suspicions". She is consumed by this need to please and maintain a sense of purity, but Clarissa's discontent is deep-seated and can not be suppressed.

Clarissa goes to find the dress she will wear this evening. It has been torn and needs mending as someone had trod on the skirt. She was fond of the rarity of the dress as it had been made by Sally Parker just before she retired. It provided her with a sense of importance and separated her from other people. She wants nothing more than to be desired, spoken about, and **revered**. Lucy offers to help mend the dress. Clarissa repeatedly thanks her as she knows how busy Lucy is with the preparations. Clarissa's servants appear to like her and believe she treats them with respect and dignity.

Revered: to be greatly respected and admired.

Clarissa returns to a sense of calmness and reflects on the nature of life as "waves collect, overbalance, and fall; collect and fall; and the whole world seems to be saying 'that is all.'" The imagery of the rhythmic pattern of waves and the ocean offers reassurance and comfort to Clarissa. She is provided a sense of certainty which she likens to the heart "which sighs collectively for all sorrows, and renews, begins, collects, lets fall." The heart is a metaphor for life and the alternating periods of joy and suffering that characterises life.

Suddenly a man arrives and demands to see Clarissa. She flees upstairs and attempts to hide her dress "like a virgin protecting chastity, respecting privacy." This reflects her vulnerability and the way she seeks to hide her inner self from the world. Clarissa greatly values her privacy and the control It gives her. The man followed her upstairs and we learn that it is Peter Walsh. He has returned from India and is amused by the way Clarissa is mending her dress. He feels that she has become more irritated and agitated. Peter believes there to be nothing worse for women than marriage, politics, and a conservative husband.

Clarissa finds Peter "enchanting" and she is reminded of the way she rejected his desire to marry her. That rejection had caused in Peter immense grief "which rose like a moon looked at from a terrace, ghastly beautiful with light from the sunken day." The imagery creates a sense of hopelessness in Peter that has persisted within him, constantly resurfacing like a moon.

They reminisce on the old times at Bourton: about how the blinds would flap, how her father never liked him, and about the lake. Clarissa remembers feeding bread to ducks at the lake as a child with her parents. It was a much simpler time, and as she fed the ducks, she "grew larger and larger in her arms, until it became a whole life, a complete life." Yet she feels that her life is incomplete and lacks meaning. She questions where she is today as Peter questions whether he should tell Clarissa about Daisy.

Peter chooses to tell Clarissa about his love for Daisy, a girl he met in India. Daisy is currently married to a Major in the Indian Army. Daisy has two children and intends to divorce her husband for Peter. Peter has returned to London to consult with lawyers about getting her divorced so they could start a life together. Peter is overwhelmed by his emotions, and he breaks down in tears as he speaks about Daisy. Clarissa kisses his hand and now feels defeated and alone, with some regrets for rejecting Peter as "she had gone up into the tower alone and left them blackberrying in the sun." This imagery suggests that her isolation is a result of her choices, and she is now left to suffer whilst others live more freely and happily.

Peter walks to the window and peers out, his back now to Clarissa. She fantasises about running away with him and going on "some great voyage" and experiencing "five acts of a play." However, Clarissa knows she would never go through with any of this, suggesting she is hopeless and lacks the ambitions of her youth to act on her desires.

This shift from excited **escapism** to a resignation and acceptance of the **monotony** of life inhibits her growth and the path to fulfilment. Peter begins to ask "are you happy, Clarissa? Does Richard–" but is interrupted by Elizabeth entering the room. Peter goes to leave as Clarissa implores him to attend her party tonight, "having to raise her voice against the roar of the open air."

Escapism: the desire to distract oneself from unpleasant realities.

Section 4

Peter walks along Victoria Street as Clarissa's invitation repeats in his head. He is annoyed at the way Clarissa introduced Elizabeth as "here is my Elizabeth!" rather than 'here's Elizabeth.' Peter finds it insincere and thinks it is cold to speak as if she had ownership or possession of Elizabeth. Clarissa's phrasing devalues Elizabeth and reflects the way Clarissa has sought marriage and children as a way of finding fulfilment. It is an attempt to force happiness through leading a perfect a life.

Monotony: repetitive or lacking in variety and interest.

A cloud passes in front of the sun, inducing silence upon London. This silence elicits Peter's sense of emptiness as "rigid, the skeleton of habit alone upholds the human frame. Where there is nothing, Peter Walsh said to himself; feeling hollowed out, utterly empty within." This metaphor captures the way most characters interact with the world, including Clarissa; they lead typical lives of nobility and are concerned greatly with their public perception. It is all a distraction, and it is only when there is silence that they are forced to reconcile with their hollowness. Clarissa distracts herself with her parties, Richard and Elizabeth. It is when she is isolated that she must deal with her dissatisfying life and despair. Similarly, Peter is battling his feelings and is forced to come to terms with the next stage of his life.

The clock in St Margaret's church strikes to signal the time and is described as "like a hostess who comes into her drawing-room on the very stroke of the hour and finds her guests there already." The simile parallels Clarissa's natural hostess nature, representing the rigidity of her life. This devotion to being a hostess and trying to please others reflects the uncertainty within her. Despite being a natural hostess, her voice lacks confidence as it is "reluctant to inflict its individuality. Some grief for the past holds it back; some concern for the present." Clarissa's suffering deeply affects her and limits her autonomy and hence her happiness. The strikes of the bells reinforces her grief and the abandonment of her youthful dreams.

The bells remind Peter of the passing of time, how he has aged and running out of time. He fears that he may have "set, or dried in the least," highlighting his worry that it is too late for him to change and to find fulfilment. The metaphor is used to depict Peter as trapped and unable to control his fate. He reflects on his socialist youth when he was expelled from Oxford and was "in some sense a failure," though the **low modality** implies that he secretly yearns for this same passion and ambition, not regarding his former self as a true failure.

Low modal: words that convey uncertainty (e.g. some, may, could) as opposed to high modal (e.g. all, must, have to).

Peter declares that the future and civilisation "lies in the hands of young men like that." This phrase is repeated and is a central idea that Woolf is expressing. Woolf presents the solution to injustice and suffering is the bravery and daring nature of young people with the will to force change. Peter admires these youthful ambitions but has abandoned his own. He is **nostalgic** for the past and can not seem to escape thoughts of Clarissa.

Nostalgic: wistful longing for a time past.

Peter observes a group of sixteen year old boys marching in uniform. They are carrying guns and have "an expression like the letters of a legend written round the base of a statue praising duty, gratitude, fidelity, love of England." The imagery of the rounded letters and a statue represents that their beliefs are **archaic** and unrepresentative of modern society. Peter respects the boys but does not want that life for himself. Only Clarissa knows that Peter has returned to London from his voyage. He feels isolated as the earth "still seemed an island to him, the strangeness of standing alone, alive, unknown." He feels out of place and uncertain about his existence as he questions "What is it? Where am I? And why, after all, does one do it?" The rhetorical questions create a sense of **existential dread** as Peter appears to lack motivation and certainty.

Archaic: outdated and old fashioned.

Existential dread: a feeling of apprehension and fear about life, death, and mortality.

Peter is suddenly overwhelmed by a sense of energy and youth. He starts to explore London and its "endless avenues," representing the opportunities that are still available to Peter for growth. For a single hour, he feels completely free, as if he is escaping the state of uncertainty that has kept him restrained. He feels "like a child who runs out of doors", evoking images of innocence and naivety as the escape is nothing more than a short **reprieve** from his crisis of identity.

Reprieve: a brief rest or relief from an unpleasant situation.

Peter follows a woman down many streets who he remarks has "a dignity about her. She was not worldly, like Clarissa; not rich, like Clarissa." This shows Peter's attachment to genuine experiences and authentic people. He views Clarissa as having been corrupted and distorted by her obsession with wealth and status. He continues to follow the woman until she enters a building and locks the door. The nameless woman represents Peter's **anguish** as his ambitions have never come to fruition. Like the woman, they are an enticing fantasy but locked away – unreachable and unobtainable. The moment of exhilaration is now over and "was smashed to atoms."

Anguish: severe mental distress or suffering.

Peter now walks to Regent's Park and is mesmerised by the city of London. Despite always being opposed to the concept of empires and armies, he feels sentimental and civilisation "seemed dear to him as a personal possession; moments of pride in England." Peter is amazed by the complexity of civilisation and how "wholly admirable, good fellows" people go about their lives each day and the form the base of society that allows it to prosper.

Peters sits down to rest as he is drowsy and has lost the energy he had a moment ago when he chased that woman. His lack of energy is juxtaposed with the movement of London, "moving branches, children's voices, the shuffle of feet, and people passing, and humming traffic, rising and falling traffic." The imagery highlights the active and busy nature of society which contrasts Peter's **lethargy** and inaction. He drifts off to sleep: "down, down he sank into the plumes and feathers of sleep, sank, and was muffled over." This line portrays Peter's loneliness and position as an outsider. It becomes clear that Clarissa's imagining of Peter as a free individual and an adventurer is not completely true. Peter is still affected by the pain of Clarissa's rejection and his inability to move past her.

Lethargy: a lack of energy, sluggishness.

Section 5

Now asleep, Peter dreams about a solitary traveller involving multiple women. It appears that the solitary traveller is Peter. There is a woman who is made of sky and branches with "magnificent hands" that showed compassion. He continues down the path and encounters a second woman. The woman is elderly and who appears "to seek, over a desert, a lost son; to search for a rider destroyed." He walks further down a village street past women knitting and men digging in the garden. The last woman he sees is a landlady who asks him if there is anything else he needs. The solitary traveller is unsure "to whom does the solitary traveller make reply?"

The dream represents Peter's journey and his uncertainty. The dream is hazy and unclear but suggests Peter is suffering and alienated. The visions "proffer great **cornucopias** full of fruit to the solitary traveller, or murmur in his ear like **sirens** serves as a warning about the potential to be consumed by dreams as a way to escape one's present reality. Woolf is critical of this inaction and represents one's unwillingness to act on their dreams as detrimental to their sense of purpose.

Peter is allured by women and their beauty. He is currently conflicted between his current lover Daisy and his past passionate love for Clarissa. The women in his dream reflect his belief that finding the right woman will remedy his suffering and cause happiness. The hesitation and lack of response to the nal question in the dream reflects the great uncertainty Peter faces and ests that he can not be saved from his suffering without dealing with t causes of his pain.

es to proclaim "the death of the soul." The words remind him of t Bourton in the early 1890s during summer. We flashback to f people including Clarissa, Peter, and Sally were talking. At madly in love with Clarissa. Clarissa was telling the group ied his housemaid. Clarissa mocked the housemaid for essed "like a cockatoo."

Cornucopias: a hollow goat's horn overflowing with fruit – an ancient traditional symbol of abundance.

Sirens: a creatures in Greek mythology that lured sailors into shipwrecks by charming, seductive singing.

Sally spoke up to say that they only married after having a baby. Clarissa is shocked by this and continues to mock the woman. At the time, having a child outside of marriage was seen to be an act of shame and embarrassment by society. Peter disliked her attitude and thought she appeared "timid; hard; something arrogant; unimaginative; prudish". He knew that Clarissa's behaviour was due to her sheltered life, but he declared that her intolerance and unsympathetic nature was "the death of the soul." The people around were uncomfortable symbolised through the image of "the whole party sitting round the tea-table seemed to wobble." An embarrassed Clarissa walked away alone.

Peter reflects on how they would often communicate like this without words. She would know by his look that he was criticising and challenging her. They often alternate between periods of quarrelling and periods of friendship and making up. That night had left Peter feeling quite gloomy as was not able to see her. Peter's passionate love for Clarissa causes him great grief as he is often unable to get past her "impenetrability."

That same night was when Clarissa had first met Richard Dalloway. Richard was new to Bourton and joined them as they had dinner. Peter and Clarissa were not talking that night and Peter ate quietly as "everything seemed to race past him; he just sat there, eating." This emphasises how deeply in love Peter is with Clarissa as he views nothing else as important or worth his time. He noticed that Clarissa was talking to Richard and he immediately knew that Clarissa would go on to marry him. Peter's jealousy and dejection pained him as he was "prey to revelations." The image of prey portrays Peter as a victim of his love and desire for Clarissa. It also suggests he lacks the power to act on his love for Clarissa, subjecting him to a state of loneliness and longing that can not be fulfilled.

Richard was seated with Aunt Helena, a traditional and typical figure of English society. She is emblematic of the restrictive social norms, hence is shocked and appalled by Sally's reckless behaviour. Richard's placement next to Aunt Helena contrasts him to Peter. Richard is a more conventional man, well-adapted to the society of the time. This makes him a much safer choice for Clarissa than Peter. Peter realised this and became quite **irate** and jealous. His anger caused him to call Clarissa "the perfect hostess" which he knew would insult and upset her.

Irate: a feeling of great anger, annoyance, or irritability.

At the end of dinner, Sally suggested they all take a boat ride on the la Initially, Peter stays behind talking with Aunt Helena as he is too devast to accompany them to the lake, feeling abandoned and hurt by Cla However, Clarissa returned to invite Peter to join them. This caused im elation for Peter who then experienced "twenty minutes of perfect hap Clarissa and Peter had a strange relationship as Richard began to fa with and **court** Clarissa.

Court: and old-fashioned word for dating someone with the intention to marry them.

Clarissa and Peter had a special, intimate bond that went beyond words as "they went in and out of each other's minds without any effort." Despite this, Peter resigned himself to the belief that Clarissa would marry Richard Dalloway. He thought it was his fault for being too unconventional, emotional, and absurd.

As Clarissa began to fall in love with Richard, her relationship with Peter strained. Clarissa began to change and was retreating from the more free-spirited nature she had developed with Sally. On one occasion, Sally had made a joke about Richard (a joke which she had made many times before). Clarissa could no longer stand it and she "suddenly stiffened, coloured, in a way she had, and **rapped** out sharply, "we've had enough of that feeble joke." Her sudden outburst towards Sally shows the abandonment of their love and connection. Woolf is representing the choice for a conventional life of mundanity as **incongruent** with individuality.

Rapped: to say something loudly and quickly.

Incongruent: not compatible.

Peter became desperate that summer and had difficulty sleeping as Clarissa drifted further and further from the woman Peter loved. He viewed her as sacrificing all that was important in life for the security and safety of a man like Richard. Peter asked Clarissa to meet him by the fountain far from the house and surrounded by trees and shrubbery. Their meeting was especially tense as "they stood with the fountain between them, the spout (it was broken) dribbling water incessantly." The fountain between them is a physical barrier which symbolises their growing disconnection and conflicting values. The incessant dripping of water further creates tension and reflects the magnitude of the moment. The broken fountain suggests that their relationship has become dysfunctional and harmful for both Clarissa and Peter.

Peter repeatedly begged Clarissa to tell him the truth about the way she felt. He was frustrated with her lack of honesty and emotions and "he felt as if his forehead would burst. She seemed contracted, petrified. She did not move." Her lack of response is a result of her fear and insecurity of exposing her inner self. Clarissa has begun to believe that intimate expressions make one vulnerable and is bothered by Peter's sensitive nature.

Peter continued pressing, desperate for the truth so that he could understand their relationship and their future but "she was unyielding. She was like iron, like flint, rigid up the backbone." The symbolism provides insight into Clarissa's insecurity that has immobilised her and left her cold and unwilling to express herself. This is emblematic of Clarissa's desire for reputation and the nobility of the upper class. It was here where she made the decision of pursuing Richard and declared to Peter that this was the end for them. Without displaying any vulnerability or emotions, Clarissa turned and walked away. Peter cried out her name but she never returned or turned back. Peter felt crushed and could not bear to remain in Bourton. He left and never returned.

Section 6

We shift back to Septimus and Lucrezia who are still in Regent's Park. Lucrezia has left Septimus sitting alone and is walking down the path. She is questioning why she has to suffer and deal with the way Septimus is; "why tortured? Why?" She is unable to empathise with Septimus' condition and struggles to communicate with him. She suddenly feels "like a bird sheltering under the thin hollow of a leaf, who blinks at the sun when the leaf moves." This image of Lucrezia sheltering under a hollow leaf depicts her as helpless in repairing her relationship with Septimus and represents her vulnerability to the suffering of the world that has devastated Septimus and left her in despair and isolation.

Lucrezia thinks of Septimus' decaying mental state, noting that his experiences in the war were not unique and that "such things happen to every one. Every one has friends who were killed in the War." This reflects Lucrezia's confusion about the way Septimus is behaving as it is quite extreme and his experience of loss is common within society. It emphasises the widespread impacts of the war and the trauma that has persisted five years later. Lucrezia thinks of how Septimus has visions and sees and hears strange things that are not there. He has heard people talking behind the walls of their bedroom and has seen an old woman's head in the middle of a fern. His mental condition has deteriorated, and his thoughts are consumed by delusions and despair. Septimus believes that he and Lucrezia should kill themselves and believes the universe has revealed hidden truths to him. These revelations include that all people are wicked and he knows their thoughts, that trees were alive, and that love and crime do not exist.

She returns to Septimus now who is "gasping, trembling, painfully drawing out these profound truths." This imagery reflects Septimus' relationship with the world; he has become a victim of civilisation that **propagated** war and is now unable to communicate with the world that has abandoned him. These truths torture Septimus and leave him unable to distinguish between his visions and reality. Septimus is beholden to his delusions that leave his body "**macerated** until only the nerve fibres were left. It was spread like a veil upon a rock." The symbolism of being macerated represents how his trauma and inability to express his pain has eroded his consciousness. He has lost his personality and identity and is now merely nerve fibres, suggesting he has wasted away. The voices encourage Septimus to tell the world about the secrets he has learnt and to tell the Prime Minister.

Propagated: widely spread or promoted.

Macerated: softened into pulp or mash.

He quickly drifts from reality again and begins talking to himself. He struggles to break free, "to open his eyes; but a weight was on them; a fear." Septimus is gripped by the fear of what he has become – he fears he is insane and is disconnected from reality. The symbolism of his eyes being pressed shut by a weight reflects how he is absorbed by his delusions and insanity which isolates him and **exacerbates** his condition.

Exacerbate: to make a bad situation even worse.

The internal chaos facing Septimus is revealed as "the earth thrilled beneath him. Red flowers grew through his flesh; their stiff leaves rustled by his head. Music began clanging against the rocks up here." The experience is overwhelming for him, and the symbolism of music clanging and flowers growing through his flesh represents the invasive nature of his trauma. He is unable to find peace and solitude.

Lucrezia interrupts Septimus to tell him that it is time to go and see Sir William Bradshaw, a renowned and well-respected doctor who Lucrezia is hopeful will be able to treat Septimus so they can return to normal. Septimus had previously been seeing Dr Holmes who was dismissive of Septimus' condition. As Lucrezia told Septimus it was time to go, "the word 'time' split its husk; poured its riches over him; and from his lips fell like **shells**, like shavings from a plane." The allusion to war represents the internal conflict of Septimus as he grapples with reality. It creates a sense of mortality through the pressure of time and Septimus' declining mental state. This reminder of time seems to remind Septimus of the beauty of life as it "poured its riches over him," but this is undercut by his inability to express himself, especially to Lucrezia.

Shells: an artillery projectile (i.e. in this context, shells from a gun, not shells on a beach!).

Septimus thinks that his marriage with Lucrezia is finished and **irreparable**. Strangely, this is comforting to Septimus, as he felt this would set him free, "the lord of men, should be free; alone." Septimus views Lucrezia as a threat to his autonomy. She refuses to engage with his visions and the divine truths he believes he has acquired. Lucrezia consistently interrupts Septimus as he is talking to himself and tries to stifle his visions which tends to upset Septimus. It becomes clear that Septimus desperately needs help or else his insanity will take control.

Irreparable: unable to be rectified or repaired.

Septimus sees Evans again which frightens him and causes "furrows of despair on his cheeks." Evans approaches Septimus as Lucrezia tries to distract him by asking for the time. Lucrezia expresses how unhappy she is. Peter, also in the park, passes by them. He is amused by their youth and their relationship and ponders as to how they have a "look so desperate as that on a fine summer morning?" Peter reflects on his return to London and how many things have changed within London society over the five years he had been overseas. He suspects those years had been "somehow very important" in the development of London society. He notices that people seem different and women tend to wear more makeup now. He also notices that people appear to speak more openly now and newspapers can discuss subjects that had previously been shied away from.

Peter now finds London "enchanting – the softness of the distances; the richness; the greenness; the civilisation" after his time in India. Peter walks along Broad Walk (a pathway through Regent's Park for pedestrians) where he amuses himself with the thought of Sally and her change since she was younger. Sally had written Peter a letter prompted by seeing blue hydrangea flowers that had reminded her of the old days at Bourton.

He knew Sally as "the wild, the daring, the romantic Sally!" yet she seems to have given up her rebellious nature for a well-adjusted life in society. She has married a rich man and now lives in a large house near Manchester.

Peter is surprised by Sally's incredible change and wonders what caused it. He remembers how Sally used to see through the nobility of Hugh Whitbread like he did. Sally believed Hugh had no inner substance and thought of nothing but his own appearance. At one point, Sally had an outburst towards Hugh who she said "represented all that was most **detestable** in British middle-class life" during a discussion at Bourton about women's rights. Hugh encapsulated the **narcissism** of the aristocracy that Hugh adored.

Detestable: abhorrent, hateful, or loathsome.

Narcissism: self-centred and selfish.

Sally had claimed that Hugh had tried to kiss her once. She insisted it had happened, but other people doubted that the respectable Hugh would try to kiss someone like Sally. We do not get a conclusive answer as to whether Hugh did try to kiss Sally; if he did, it could be seen as a desire of Hugh to break free from his superficiality, though Sally believed "the stable boys had more life in them than Hugh," reflecting how the pursuit of reputation and nobility corrodes one's desires for individuality. Woolf uses Hugh to represent this depressing nature and to highlight how out of touch the aristocrats are with society.

Hugh had married the Honourable Evelyn and found a job at court. They lived a wealthy life in one of the "pompous houses overlooking [Regent's] Park." Peter needs a job now that he is back in London and intends on asking either Hugh or Richard to help set him up with something. Peter likes Richard's character, his "sensible way; without a touch of imagination, without a spark of brilliancy, but with the inexplicable niceness of his type." He describes Richard as a little dull, but a genuine person. It is this **ingenuity** that Peter despises in Hugh. Peter thinks Richard's good nature is "wasted on politics."

Ingenuity: being clever or innovative.

Peter thinks back to when Clarissa was falling in love with Richard. Peter implored Sally to save Clarissa "from the Hughs and the Dalloways and all the other "perfect gentlemen" who would "stifle her soul... make a mere hostess of her, encourage her worldliness." Peter fears that Clarissa will be absorbed by the world that inhibits and **scorns** individual expression. The symbol of the hostess represents the decay of one's soul through a shallowness and total concern for the superficiality of presentation and appearance. Woolf characterises the desire for perfection as sacrificing and giving up the authenticity of humanity. It distorts one's individuality and replaces it with conformity that is not **conducive** of fulfilment.

Scorns: to feel contempt or disdain for something.

Conducive: conditions that lead to a desirable outcome.

Peter depicts Clarissa as a seemingly ordinary woman but with a special gift of drawing the attention of all as "it was Clarissa one remembered. Not that she was striking; not beautiful at all; there was nothing picturesque about her; she never said anything specially clever; there she was, however; there she was." The image of Clarissa portrays her as mystifying as she has this significant social presence and charm despite a lack of distinguishing features or personality. We see Clarissa's transformation into the perfect hostess and the abandonment of her youthful ambitions. However, her youthful self is intertwined with her present self and is unable to be suppressed.

Peter attempts to justify to himself that he is no longer in love with Clarissa. He tells himself that he is only thinking about her to try to understand her. He is "unable to get away from the thought of her; she kept coming back and back like a sleeper jolting against him in a railway carriage." The railway carriage is metaphoric of how Peter can not escape her; they are bound together, and Peter must deal with his past and present feelings. The imagery created of jolting represents Peter's internal disarray as he tries to understand his feelings. He is consumed by the thought of Clarissa and is unable to reconcile his feelings, leaving him bitter and dejected. It is impossible for Peter to remove Clarissa from his mind, suggesting he is still in love with her and that one's past is inescapable.

Peter reflects on the death of Clarissa's sister, Sylvia, who was killed by a falling tree – an event that Clarissa witnessed. This is the only mention of Sylvia's death and it is from Peter's perspective. Initially, Clarissa was mad at God. She later became an atheist which guided her morality as "evolved this atheist's religion of doing good for the sake of goodness." As a result, Clarissa seemed to have "no bitterness in her; none of that sense of moral virtue which is so repulsive in good women." Peter's comments reflect that Clarissa has the potential for the exciting and fulfilling life she desires.

Instead, Clarissa "**frittered** her time away, lunching, dining, giving these incessant parties of hers." Clarissa's **facade** and need for people to desire and revere her has tarnished the youthful Clarissa, removing her individuality and replacing it with the image of nobility and class. Peter notes that there are times where people bring out Clarissa's vitality and comedy but these are increasingly rare. Clarissa's parties represent her prioritisation of her public exterior and the way she distracts herself from her dissatisfaction. Her parties are "blunting the edge of her mind, losing her discrimination." Peter views growing old differently to Clarissa. He believes old age involves acquiring the experience needed to take hold of one's passions to evoke the "full flavour; to extract every ounce of pleasure, every shade of meaning". He believes one's youth is full of passion and ambition but lacks the experience to apply this in a meaningful and practical way.

Frittered: to waste one's time doing meaningless things.

Façade: a false or deceptive outward appearance.

Ruminating: to think deeply and repetitively.

Indifferent: a lack of interest or concern.

Peter notices he spends hours and days **ruminating** over Clarissa but does not think of Daisy much. He feels that his persistent love for Clarissa has deteriorated him and "reduced him to – a whimpering, snivelling old ass." Peter feels that he is trapped by his emotions and is bothered by how Clarissa seems so calm and **indifferent** towards him now. Their reunion has made Peter question his sensitivity as Clarissa was so focused on her dress and "was as cold as an icicle."

Peter and Clarissa are inseparable and are both dealing with perceived inadequacy and unhappiness. Woolf portrays Clarissa's development as incomplete as she can not completely free herself of her past. Her past is inescapable and bound to her identity, and these competing states causes Clarissa's suffering. She can not be the perfect hostess with a secure life of safety whilst also having deep-seated aspirations and desires for freedom. Therefore, Woolf takes the reader into the world of Clarissa to encourage reflection on one's own nature and battle for control.

Peter hears an old woman singing, "the voice of an ancient spring spouting from earth... like a wind-beaten tree." The lyrics are indecipherable but appears to be singing some universal message about the world. She is begging for change and "would still be there in ten million years." This suggests that the world never really changes, and everyone is subjected to the will of the universe. Peter pities the "poor creature" and gives her a coin as he gets into his taxi.

Derision: to mock, ridicule, or scoff at.

The perspective now shifts to Septimus and Lucrezia who are waiting to cross and also hear the woman singing. Whilst Peter reacts with pity, Lucrezia reacts with **derision** to the "poor old wretch!" Lucrezia is taking Septimus to see Sir William Bradshaw, whose name she liked, with the hope that he would be able to cure Septimus.

Pervasive: widespread and found all throughout.

Septimus is depicted as a victim and alienated by society, left to fend for himself as "London has swallowed up many millions of young men called Smith; thought nothing of fantastic Christian names like Septimus with which their parents have thought to distinguish them." The typical name of Smith symbolises the **pervasive** nature of his struggles and suppression. By contrast, the more unique name of Septimus implies a sense of individuality, yet Septimus' condition is ignored and dismissed. This suggests that society has no concern for people like Septimus that do not represent value through wealth or power.

Predispose: to make someone more inclined to an attitude, action, or condition.

Septimus looks like a typical man but is deeply suffering and is never at peace. Like most people, he "has flowered; flowered from vanity, ambition, idealism, passion, loneliness, courage, laziness, the usual seeds." The metaphor of flowering emphasises that society's lack of empathy and care **predisposes** individuals to enduring and unrelenting suffering with no hope of escape. This makes it incredibly difficult to break free and find fulfilment.

This is particularly evident in the war where immense loss and suffering was inflicted on all those involved as "so prying and insidious were the fingers of the European War, smashed a plaster cast of **Ceres**, ploughed a hole in the geranium beds." The metaphor emphasises the loss of humanity that war causes and the insidious impacts that persist. The hole suggests permanent damage with no path for returning to normality.

Ceres: the ancient Roman goddess of agriculture.

The sacrifices that soldiers like Septimus made in securing victory for Britain deserved admiration and gratitude, however, Septimus and others were abandoned and their illnesses swiftly ignored. With little understanding of mental health at the time, those experiencing PTSD were largely seen to be cowards and lacking the will and mental fortitude to deal with trauma. We flashback to Septimus' experiences in and immediately after the war. Septimus had eagerly volunteered when the war began. He fought in the trenches in France and was an excellent soldier. He was quickly promoted by his officer, Evans, with whom he shared a great bond through their service in the war. Evans was tragically killed just before the **armistice** in November 1918. His experiences had greatly changed Septimus and he lacked the passion and excitement he had when enlisting for the war. "He was right there. The last shells missed him. He watched them explode with indifference." The truncated sentences express the blunt reality that Septimus had lost motivation and a purpose and was now filled with despair.

Armistice: a ceasefire or agreement to stop fighting in a war.

After the armistice, Septimus was in Milan, Italy, where he met Lucrezia. They got engaged soon after which was when Septimus first began to notice how emotionally numb he felt. He was gripped by "these sudden thunder-claps of fear. He could not feel... something failed him; he could not feel." Here, the repetition and metaphor represent the magnitude of his loss of sensations and led to Septimus believing that the world lacked meaning. Lucrezia was all he cared for, but they became more distanced and less involved as his condition worsened.

Septimus became increasingly bitter, and we learn that his perception of Shakespeare and his plays had changed drastically since before the war. He believed Shakespeare despised humanity and the mundanity of life. He developed a **nihilistic** view of the world and believed that "the secret signal which one generation passes, under disguise, to the next is loathing, hatred, despair." He was overwhelmed by a sense of sadness and indifference to the world. Lucrezia was excited about having children with Septimus but he thought "one cannot bring children into a world like this. One cannot perpetuate suffering, or increase the breed of these lustful animals, who have no lasting emotions, but only whims and vanities." The extent of his personal suffering has left him with a bleak view of humanity, believing that humans lack kindness and charity.

Nihilistic: the belief that life has no meaning.

This sense of humanity lacking of purpose and morality is furthered through the dehumanisation of how humans "hunt in packs. Their packs scour the desert and vanish screaming into the wilderness. They desert the fallen. They are plastered over with **grimaces**." This represents humans as uncaring and individualistic with no binding goodness. This decay in Septimus is a result of his experiences in the war compounded with his lack of support, acknowledgement, and feeling.

Grimace: an ugly facial expression to convey disgust or pain.

We return to the present day in 1923. Lucrezia weeps as she feels unhappy, alone and fears she will never have children. Septimus hears her cries but is unfazed by her raw emotions as "he felt nothing" and "descended another step into the pit." The imagery of a pit mirrors the emptiness Septimus faces as his love and humanity is fading, leaving him as a hollow shell of his former self. Septimus is now completely demoralised and surrenders to his condition as he "mechanically and with complete consciousness of its insincerity, he dropped his head on his hands... He gave in." The image of a mechanical motion reflects how Septimus is devoid of life and completely disconnected from humanity.

We now see recent events where Lucrezia sought help for Septimus' condition. Dr Holmes, a general practitioner, had been seeing Septimus but believed there was nothing particularly wrong with Septimus, declaring that "health is largely a matter in our own control." This dismissive attitude made Lucrezia more confused and Septimus more isolated. Septimus views Dr Holmes as an oppressive force punishing Septimus for his numbness. When Dr Holmes had returned another day, Septimus refused to see him. He forced his way in anyway and accused Septimus of being too selfish and making Lucrezia fret with worry. Dr Holmes continued to visit each day despite Septimus resenting his attempts at intervention. This confused Lucrezia further as she believed Dr Holmes was nice and had good intentions. In reality, Dr Holmes reinforces Septimus' beliefs about the repulsiveness of humanity which only worsens his state of mind. Septimus felt completely deserted by Lucrezia and his thoughts of suicide returned as "the whole world was clamouring: Kill yourself, kill yourself, for our sakes." This emphasises the fragility of Septimus' mind and how the inner upheaval he faces is overwhelming. He does not want to die but is unable to communicate his suffering with the world or Lucrezia.

Delirious: a disturbed or incoherent state of mind.

Admonish: to reprimand or scold someone for doing something wrong.

Whilst Lucrezia was out shopping one day, Evans appeared to Septimus again. Lucrezia returned to find Septimus **delirious** and was "wild with terror, for he was talking to himself." She immediately sent for Dr Holmes who **admonished** Septimus for frightening Lucrezia. Dr Holmes said that if they were unhappy with his work, they could go and see Sir William Bradshaw instead.

Section 7

This scene starts with the striking of Big Ben, dividing the day and reminding us of the passing of time. Big Ben's "stroke was wafted over the northern part of London; blent with that of other clocks, mixed in a thin **ethereal** way with the clouds and wisps of smoke." The symbolism of the clocks merging emphasises the progression of time that can never be controlled or limited. Likewise the imagery of the sound wafting, mixing with clouds and smoke creates an ominous atmosphere which places stress onto the characters as they struggle between fulfilment and conformity whilst facing the endless pressure of time and ageing.

Ethereal: delicate, spiritual, and seemingly not of this world.

Clarissa has finished mending her dress and is preparing for her party. She finds pleasure from her role within society as a hostess that brings people together. This contrasts with Septimus who is exposed and condemned by society for his illness and perceived cowardice. Septimus and Lucrezia arrive at Sir William Bradshaw's house. He is well-known for treating the wealthy and charges high fees, often travelling to the country for his well-off patients.

Sir William had been knighted for his abilities and service to the community. He had an incredible reputation "not merely of lightning skill, and almost infallible accuracy in diagnosis but of sympathy; tact; understanding of the human soul." The introduction of Sir William with emphasis on his skill and sympathy gives the impression that he is understanding, genuine and compassionate. This reputation is what had attracted Lucrezia as she felt someone more sympathetic and gentler may help to alleviate Septimus' suffering. Despite this, his diagnosis shows a lack of empathy and a sense of **hubris** that stifles patients.

Hubris: excessive self-confidence or pride.

As soon as Sir William sees Septimus, he is certain "it was a case of extreme gravity. It was a case of complete breakdown." Sir William is dismayed by Dr Holmes' assessment that there is nothing wrong with Septimus. He notes that half of his time is spent attempting to undo the mistakes of general practitioners like Dr Holmes. He questions if Septimus had served in the war and asks Lucrezia if he has threatened to take his own life. Septimus struggles to remember the war and describes it as "that little **shindy** of schoolboys with gunpowder." This emphasises the tragedy of the war through the image of schoolboys losing their innocence and decimated by conflict and loss. Lucrezia answers for Septimus and says that "he served with the greatest distinction" and was even promoted. Lucrezia chooses to speak for Septimus and attempts to silence him as he tries to say he has committed a crime against humanity. This is due to the shame of mental illness at the time which Lucrezia wants to avoid.

Shindy: a loud disturbance or quarrel.

Sir William recognises the extent of Septimus' condition but fails to address it sufficiently due to the lack of experience and understanding of mental illness at the time. He decides quite quickly on how to treat Septimus with no consultation with him or Lucrezia. Sir William declares that he will send Septimus to a house in the country to give him a chance to get what he needs, "rest, rest, rest; a long rest in bed." Lucrezia is upset by his suggestion and finds it horrible that he recommends Lucrezia stay away from Septimus as he recovers. Sir William argues that loved ones are not good around people as they recover.

This treatment of rest and isolation was the same that Woolf had experienced with her mental illness. Woolf believed this seclusion from the world and intellectual stimulation to be maddening. As Woolf herself saw specialists to treat her condition, one had encouraged her to practise **equanimity**. This appears to have inspired Sir William Bradshaw's mantra of reclaiming "a sense of proportion." Here, proportion is a **callous** way of describing a state where feeling and emotions are repressed. It represents the authority of British society that alienates those who do not fit neatly within society. Septimus is describes as "the most **exalted** of mankind; the criminal who faced his judges; the victim exposed on the heights; the fugitive; the drowned sailor." This imagery captures the vulnerability of Septimus and how his illness is shamed. The emphasis of the judge, victim, and fugitive reflects the cruelty of Sir William and how he abuses his patients. The archetype of doctors as sympathetic, caring, and patient is undermined by Sir William's worldview and the power he wields.

Equanimity: a state of calmness and composure under stress.

Callous: cruel or insensitive.

Exalted: of a high rank or held in high regard.

Sir William discusses how everyone gets depression and impulses. He simplifies the issue and fails to understand Septimus which inhibits any rehabilitation. Septimus is left tormented by his mind as "once you fall, Septimus repeated to himself, human nature is on you. Holmes and Bradshaw are on you." The lack of help or sympathy leaves Septimus viewing the doctors as enemies attempting to silence him. Septimus struggles to speak and stammers on his words. He is defeated and declares "human nature is remorseless." Woolf's portrayal of Dr Holmes and Sir William Bradshaw accentuates the notion that those with power may not always have good intentions and may oppress those beneath them.

Lucrezia feels deserted by Sir William as she wanted Septimus to be helped, not sent away for weeks. Sir William refuses to engage with his patients. He does not see them as capable of change, but merely inferiors that need to be sent away. Despite Septimus' decaying mind, he is not beyond rehabilitation. He is desperate to communicate his internal struggle and his suffering but has difficulty expressing himself. Septimus is discouraged by society and the doctors from individual expression, leaving him silenced.

Even Lucrezia who loves him dearly shows a sense of embarrassment about Septimus' state of mind and feels the need to explain his bravery in combat to Sir William. This lack of communication and expression seems to be central to Woolf's message. Woolf suggests communication is the key to staying in touch with one's humanity and ensuring a fulfilling life.

Sir William is presented as a man consumed by the power and authority he has over his patients. He has a **methodical** approach to his patients that does not change based on individual circumstances or need. This uniform approach involves viewing his patients as scorns of society and burdens. He took great pride in his work as he "not only prospered himself but made England prosper, secluded her lunatics, forbade childbirth, penalised despair." Sir William sought to preserve social order by abhorrent methods that gave him pleasure and tormented his patients. Woolf challenges the idea of a prosperous nation if it **denigrates** and oppresses its citizens in this way.

Methodical: done in an orderly way and according to established procedure.

Denigrate: belittle and disparage.

Sir William imposed his values onto his patients with no regard to their humanity as he "made it impossible for the unfit to propagate their views until they, too, shared his sense of proportion." Sir William is the embodiment of the corruption of power. He reflects the tendency of those with authority to abuse it and subject their will onto those with less power. Sir William seeks to cover up the flaws of society as its victims are removed from public view.

This sense of power is furthered through Sir William's obsession with conversion, what he calls proportion's "sister, less smiling, more formidable, a Goddess." This reflects Sir William's worldview as he pursues proportion and conversion. This pursuit blinds him to the genuine needs of his patients. Conversion "feasts on the wills of the weakly, loving to impress, to impose, adoring her own features stamped on the face of the populace." The metaphor of conversion stamping its features onto the population emphasises the suppression of individuality, expression and freedom. The values of English society are imposed on its people with any deviation seen as shameful.

Those who refuse to convert are sent away and made to feel worthless and are filled with despair. Conversion is the manipulation of the **innate** desires for freedom and control and the quest to turn people into obedient subjects. Sir William upholds the traditions of English society. Woolf criticises these values and exposes the incompatibility of this conformity with human nature.

Innate: naturally occurring, intrinsic.

Sir William's power has corrupted him and blinded him to the unbearable suffering of his patients. Their desperation for their pain to be alleviated left them "naked, defenceless" as Sir William "swooped; he devoured. He shut people up." This represents Sir William's detestable nature and the vulnerability of his patients. His lack of compassion, tolerance, and empathy towards his patients reflects the indifference of society to the lower class. Despite, Septimus' service and contribution to the war effort, he is alienated and made to feel undeserving of help and responsible for his own suffering.

Motif: a recurring idea or symbol.

Septimus is now completely defeated. He believes no hope remains and that he is beyond rehabilitation. This is emphasised through the **motif** of time "shredding and slicing, dividing and subdividing." The mechanical nature of time symbolises the inescapable reality of time passing and its pressure on individuals to conform and convert. Time creates a sense of despair and mortality as "the clocks of Harley Street nibbled at the June day, counselled submission, upheld authority, and pointed out in chorus the supreme advantages of a sense of proportion." The clocks reinforce the rigid structure of society and the immense authority of those in power. This paralyses Septimus and Lucrezia who are denied support and their individuality and connection suppressed in favour of the social order.

The passage ends with the sounds of the clocks and with Lucrezia crying as they leave Sir William's house. Lucrezia does not like Sir Williams and finds him unsympathetic to Septimus.

Section 8

Innocuous: harmless and inoffensive.

In this next part of the text, we see Lady Bruton's lunch party that Clarissa felt excluded from. The lunch party includes Lady Bruton, Richard Dalloway, and Hugh Whitbread, who engage in seemingly **innocuous** small talk, though we get substantial insight into them through the stream of consciousness style.

Hugh is seen walking to Lady Bruton's house. He is looking through a shop window, a habit of his. Hugh appears to embody the "proportion" that Sir William encourages. Hugh is depicted as superficial and lacking depth as "he did not go deeply. He brushed surfaces." His internal monologue is quite dull and is limited to his actions and thoughts of himself. This emphasises how he has sacrificed individuality for an appearance of nobility and importance.

Hugh is the first to arrive and brings carnations for Lady Bruton. Milly Brush, Lady Bruton's secretary, lets him in and Hugh asks how her brother is doing in South Africa. Miss Brush answers that he is doing very well, thoguh in reality, her brother has actually "been doing badly in Portsmouth." Miss Brush resents Hugh and believes him to be "one of the greediest men she had ever known." Richard arrives just after, and Lady Bruton notes that she prefers Richard as he is "made of much finer material," which suggests that Hugh's obsession with his status is off-putting. Richard is more genuine and seems to be a good person uncorrupted by ego.

Adept: to be skilled or proficient at something.

The lunch is carefully planned, and everything is set up perfectly, with the "soundless and exquisite passing to and fro through swing doors of aproned white-capped maids, handmaidens not of necessity, but **adepts** in a mystery or grand deception practised by hostesses." The imagery presents the upper class's concern for superiority and perfection. The deception is the way the lunch is designed to minimise the thoughts of or engagement with the servants – servants should be soundless and in the background, reinforcing the social hierarchy.

One of Lady Bruton's ancestors was a military general and his portrait was prominently on display. Richard remarks that Lady Bruton, along with the other women in her family, seem to look like their general ancestor. This symbolises Lady Bruton's deviation from typical femininity. Richard admires Lady Bruton and likens her to the quality of a general. He would be happy to serve under Lady Bruton's leadership.

Lady Bruton "had the reputation of being more interested in politics than people; of talking like a man." Lady Bruton has created a respectable life within the boundaries of society but appears to long for greater involvement in public society. The rigid role of women at the time prevented this, with the comparison of talking like a man furthering her repression. Whilst Lady Bruton is **affluent** and has enormous privilege, she is not immune to the controls that society has inflicted upon women.

Affluent: wealthy and prosperous.

Clarissa believes that Lady Bruton does not like her and deliberately excludes her. In some ways, Lady Bruton is the **antithesis** of Clarissa. Lady Bruton is "more interested in politics than people" whereas Clarissa is more interested in people than politics. They both struggle with their individual desires in a world that stifles individual expression, leaving the audience to reflect on how one should act in a restrictive society. Lady Bruton believes that Clarissa may have prevented Richard from advancing in his political career, particularly through her illness that took them away from London.

Antithesis: the polar opposite.

Lady Bruton asks Richard, "how's Clarissa?" This is a seemingly ordinary question that helps make polite conversation, but it appears deeper than that. Lady Bruton's question unites her with Clarissa "in a singular bond" despite the uncertainty about their relationship. It is a signal from "an almost silent companion... signified recognition of some feminine comradeship which went beneath masculine lunch parties." The relegation of women to domestic life often alienates them and can be unfulfilling. Lady Bruton's attempt to connect with Clarissa shows her feminist nature and desire for the improvement of opportunities and freedoms for women.

Hugh mentions that he had seen Clarissa that morning in the park. The conversation immediately switches to Peter Walsh as Lady Bruton mentions that he has returned to London. They all remember Peter as the man who was rejected by Clarissa and who fled to India and "come a **cropper**." Miss Brush wonders why Richard seems to hesitate and appears uneasy at the mention of Peter. Miss Brush was absorbed by these moments of silence and she participated in the "reflections of a detached spirit, of an uncorrupted soul whom life could not **bamboozle**." This characterises Peter as still having the emotional sensitivity of the soul that society sought to subdue. Lady Bruton indicates that she wants the coffee quickened.

Cropper: someone who has suffered misfortune or failure.

Bamboozle: to trick or deceive.

They reflect on Peter's unsuccessful life and how "he had come back, battered, unsuccessful, to their secure shores." Peter has returned to London to seek help from lawyers about getting Daisy divorced, yet he is still captured by the charm of Clarissa and his nostalgic sentiments. They view Peter as suffering from some sort of weakness that could not be overcome as they believe "there was some flaw in his character." Peter's refusal to conform to society's expectations leaves him feeling alone but allows him to stay well-connected to his emotions. This is unthinkable to the elites who value safety and reputation above individualism.

Peter's sad and underwhelming return is "vaguely flattering to them all." This represents how detestable the upper class can be and how insecure they are. They are constantly looking for reassurance that their lives are worthwhile, and their decisions were correct. Peter reinforces their choices for security and safety as his failure is seen to be a result of his unwillingness to preserve tradition. Peter solidifies their "secure shores" and removes some of their doubt and uncertainty.

Whilst talking about Peter, Richard thinks of how he loves Clarissa. He commits to going to her after lunch and telling her that he loves her. Lady Bruton thinks about how Hugh has become slower and fatter compared to Richard who always seemed more active and livelier. This contrast represents the physical manifestation of Richard's genuine nature compared to Hugh's artificial appearance that wears away at his soul.

Lady Bruton is becoming impatient with the state of her life in old age. Lady Bruton is not aware of the cause of these feelings and does not truly acknowledge them, but they exist within her. This creates a sense of deep discontent that she "feels rise within her, once youth is past, and must eject upon some object – it may be **Emigration**, it may be **Emancipation**." This need for a cause reflects Lady Bruton's discomfort and dissatisfaction. She finds a sense of purpose through directing her efforts towards promoting emigration to Canada.

Emigration: to move to a new country.

Emancipation: to be set free from restriction or enslavement.

Emigration represents an escape from one's problems and freedom from a changing society that threatens the upper class's stranglehold. As Lady Bruton has aged and her youth has faded, she has acquired a better understanding and appreciation of what freedom means to her. She finds emigration appealing through its offer of liberation and promotes it among the wealthy.

Lady Bruton is seen to have "perhaps lost her sense of proportion." She is another character that appears to suffer from mental illness or feelings of unhappiness. This challenges the notion that there is a clear distinction between being sane and insane. Unlike Septimus, Lady Bruton is shielded from society's derision due to her wealth and status. Her quirks are tolerated, and she is allowed to indulge in her interests and participate in society.

Lady Bruton decides to write a letter to the editor of the *Times* daily newspaper. She struggles with the words and seeks help from Hugh who possesses "a command of language; able to put things as editors like them put." Hugh appears to understand their language, further entrenching him as an archetype of higher society. Lady Bruton receives advice from Richard whilst Hugh writes as he "marvellously reduced Lady Bruton's tangles to sense, to grammar such as the editor of the *Times*." He brings a sense of order and structure to her words and enables her to communicate her dreams of emigration. Richard believes Hugh's letter is nonsensical and overdone, but Lady Bruton loves the way it is written. She is extremely appreciative of their help and takes solace in the hope that her message will spread and move others.

As Richard goes to leave Lady Bruton's residence, he reflects on the portrait of her ancestor the general. The prominence of the portrait display emphasises the sense of ancestry and tradition. This symbolises how Lady Bruton and similar people of considerable power now seem outdated in contemporary society. They appear to lack influence and are left to suffer and grapple with their regrets and isolation. The upper echelon of society desperately clings to tradition and is unwilling to change. Woolf criticises this rigidity of tradition, which is furthered through the foreshadowing of the Conservative government's upcoming defeat and replacement with the Labour Party. Richard acknowledges this inevitability and chooses to focus on doing some good with the political power he has.

Richard asks if Lady Bruton is going to attend Clarissa's party. She is unsure and has not decided yet as she is terrified of parties. Lady Bruton retreats to her room to rest which represents how she feels insecure and isolated by society. She appears to live solely through her dreams of emigration and the temporary alleviation of her pain through this. Lady Bruton is unwilling to act on these aspirations for freedom, so she is ultimately left disoriented and **melancholic**.

Melancholic: overcome with pensive, wistful sadness.

Lady Bruton is overcome by the sudden feeling of being "drowsy and heavy, drowsy and heavy, like a field of clover in the sunshine." She imagines Richard and Hugh walking through the streets, "further and further from her, being attached to her by a thin thread... which would stretch and stretch, get thinner and thinner." The metaphor of the thread emphasises the interconnectedness of the characters and the similarities between them. They all suffer from insecurity and obsessions for superficial status that leaves them unfulfilled and questioning what could have been. The sound of the bells returns and induces Lady Bruton to sleep.

The perspective now shifts to Richard who is walking along a street with Hugh. They are looking into shop windows. Hugh is excited by a Spanish necklace he sees and wants to buy for his wife, Evelyn. Richard is rather disinterested and **reluctantly** follows Hugh into the shop. Richard does not really like Hugh and does not care much for the idea of emigration or Lady Bruton's letter. Richard is attracted by "tides in the body" that compel him into the shop. The metaphor represents Richard's simplicity and how he is controlled by natural impulses and lacks the emotional sensitivity of Peter.

Reluctantly: unwilling or averse to doing something.

Richard thinks about his daughter, Elizabeth, and how she fits into society. He believes "If he'd had a boy he'd have said, Work, work. But he had his Elizabeth; he adored his Elizabeth." This reflects the pervasive gender roles within British society that oppressed both men and women. Women were largely excluded from the public sphere and denied opportunities, whereas men were pressured to be authoritative, financially secure, and **stoic**. Women were expected to maintain a sense of passivity and loyalty to family and men who expressed their emotions were seen as weak-willed. Richard loves Elizabeth but does not recognise the limitations society has placed on her.

Stoic: to resist showing emotion during hardship and suffering.

Hugh wants to see a specific worker who is familiar with Evelyn's taste in jewellery. Richard finds it strange that the worker knows Evelyn's precise measurements, which causes Richard to reflect on his relationship with Clarissa. He has very rarely shown displays of affection or romantic gestures. Richard has only ever bought a gift for Clarissa once – a bracelet that Clarissa never even wore. Clarissa and Richard's relationship **epitomises** the traditional marriages of stability and safety of the time, with passionate love not prioritised. This contrasts Clarissa's earlier relationship with Sally, and we are left to judge the importance of genuine love for one's happiness.

Epitomise: to embody or be the perfect example of something.

Richard is reminded of Peter's expressive and passionate and love for Clarissa. Richard impulsively decides to buy a gift for Clarissa to show his affection for Clarissa. Compared to Peter, Richard is a much more conventional and typical man and is emblematic of the society's ingrained culture. Peter is romantic, emotional, and unapologetically passionate. Despite Richard's more reserved nature, he genuinely loves Clarissa and Elizabeth in his own way.

Richard selects a ring that receives a poor reaction from Hugh who is being "unspeakably **pompous**." Feeling discouraged, Richard decides to leave the store as he "could not stand more than an hour of his society." Richard is at the centre of traditional British society. He is a conservative politician, has powerful friends, and has substantial wealth. Richard's dismay with his society suggests that frustration is inevitable within the society and that conforming to its demands makes a sense of fulfilment impossible. At times he despises his society, and at others he revels in it. Richard is in a conflicted state of mind where his values are incongruous with the structures he has benefited from.

Pompous: arrogant and overbearing sense of self-importance.

Richard is "eager, yes, very eager, to travel that spider's thread of attachment between himself and Clarissa; he would go straight to her." The repetition highlights Richard's excitement and desire to profess his love to Clarissa. The symbolism of the spider's thread represents his desire to reignite his relationship with Clarissa. Richard wants to unify with Clarissa and to experience the vitality of love and connection that is often absent in their marriage. Richard believes it to be a miracle that he had married Clarissa and decides to buy her flowers. He is determined to tell her how much he loves her, which he **seldom** does.

Richard reflects on the state of British society and how those "thousands of poor **chaps**, with all their lives before them, [are] shovelled together, already half forgotten." The dehumanisation reflects the way the soldiers were stripped of their identities and emphasises the **futility** of the war. Those who fought in the war were abandoned and cruelly disregarded by the elite society that initiated the war. Richard is grateful of his **fortuitous** position in life and has good intentions to enact social reform and serve the people.

Richard expresses pity towards those who are homeless and is disappointed by the way police demean them. Richard's **enviable** position in life is juxtaposed to those he pities as "our detestable social system... could be seen... as he walked across the Park to tell his wife that he loved her." This reinforces Richard's status and his immunity from the suffering that British society inflicts. Woolf criticises traditional structures that create and thrive on the immense inequality and injustice of citizens.

Richard moves towards a homeless woman and is "bearing his flowers like a weapon." This simile suggests Richard's unfamiliarity, discomfort, and his unnatural position when dealing with gestures of compassion and kindness. Conversely, Clarissa finds flowers as a source of refreshment and comfort. Richard is "considering the problem of the female **vagrant**," showing a sense of compassion that most of the upper class lack. Despite this pity, Richard actively seeks to avoid those in the lower class and sticks to those he believes are more respectable and noble.

In the past, Richard was incredibly jealous of Peter and Clarissa's relationship. Now, however, Richard is comforted by the understanding that Clarissa had chosen him as "she wanted support" and stability that Peter could not provide. She chose security and safety over the instinctive and emotional Peter; a decision that has left Clarissa in an eternal state of dread and uncertainty.

Richard notices a large crowd gathering at the gates of Buckingham Palace. The crowd appears to be waiting to see the King drive out. Richard acknowledges that Buckingham Palace has a "certain dignity" and is "a symbol, absurd though it is." The **dichotomy** between dignity and absurdity represents the hollowness of traditions and their growing insignificance.

Seldom: rarely, not often.

Chaps: British slang for men or boys.

Futility: pointless, useless, without purpose.

Fortuitous: to occur by chance and luck.

Enviable: worthy of being envied; inspiring jealousy in others.

Vagrant: a homeless beggar.

Dichotomy: a contrast between two opposing ideas or traits.

Richard is aware of the decline of the British empire, but this reality seems unnoticed by the commoners who are desperate for the attention of royalty. The attachment to the idea of royalty reflects their unfulfilled state as they find hope in meaningless and **arbitrary** symbols.

Arbitrary: based on random chance and lacking reason.

Richard's conventional nature is furthered by the description of how "he liked continuity; and the sense of handing on the traditions of the past. It was a great age in which to have lived." Despite recognising the absurdity of Buckingham Palace, he finds its symbolism comforting and important to his identity. This suggests that Richard (and the social class he represents) choose to uphold the traditional symbols because it offers security and certainty. He repeats that life is a miracle and believes that his walk to profess his love to Clarissa is the essence of true happiness.

Clarissa is agonising over whether to invite her cousin, Ellie Henderson, to her party. Ellie has expressed interest in attending, but Clarissa believes she does not fit in well with the nobility of Clarissa's parties. Clarissa questions "but why should I ask all the dull women in London to my parties?" She is fearful that Ellie would tarnish the reputation of her parties, reflecting the callous nature of Clarissa that has developed due to her insecurity and desire to please. Clarissa is also disturbed by Miss Kilman's influence on Elizabeth. Clarissa despises Miss Kilman and is uncomfortable with Elizabeth praying with her.

It is now three o'clock, indicated by the return of the bells as "the sound of Big Ben flooded Clarissa's drawing-room." The metaphor suggests that the passing of time is inescapable and creates a sense of intensity that pressures and unnerves Clarissa. Time always continues and the demands of life are ever-present; there is no chance to rest or avoid life's challenges. Clarissa is forced to deal with her internal uncertainty and suffering which can not be suppressed.

Clarissa hears "something fumbling, something scratching at the door." It is Richard, and the connotation of fumbling and scratching suggests Richard's anxiety and unease as he attempts a romantic gesture and confession of love. Richard enters holding out flowers for Clarissa which surprises her. He struggles to get out the words he wants to say and fails to tell Clarissa he loves her. Despite this, Clarissa seems to understand the gesture and is appreciative of his effort.

We now see a simple interaction between Clarissa and Richard as they discuss their day so far. They talk about how Clarissa had met with Peter and how little he had changed, and how Richard had lunch with Hugh Whitbread and Lady Bruton where they spoke about Peter. Richard mentions how Hugh has grown considerably more intolerable and how they wrote a letter to the *Times*. Clarissa complains to Richard about Ellie Henderson and Miss Kilman. Richard does not understand why Clarissa appears to care so much about her parties and says that it would be nice of her to invite Ellie.

As Richard says he must go to a committee, Clarissa reflects on the "dignity in people; a solitude; even between husband and wife a **gulf**; and that one must respect." Clarissa is exploring the idea of privacy and the importance of maintaining a private self. Marriage symbolises the union of two people, but Clarissa is emphasising the separate lives and thoughts that still exist and may conflict. Clarissa is reflecting on the nature of human consciousness; the private parts of ourselves that we hide from the world. She views this privacy as integral to staying sane and preserving one's individuality.

Gulf: a difference or division between two people.

Clarissa believes that depriving one's privacy would cause one to lose "one's independence, one's self-respect – something, after all, priceless." The reader gets an intimate view into Clarissa's mind and her internal **turmoil**. Her sense of self is fractured as she battles her youthful ambitions that resurface with her desire for certainty and stability. Woolf portrays an individual's private world as a way of finding one's identity and dealing with suffering.

Turmoil: a state of confusion, anxiety, or disturbance.

Clarissa had been quite ill and has only recently returned to normal society. Richard advises Clarissa to get an hour of rest, mimicking the doctor's previous advice for Clarissa's illness. She found this "part of his adorable, divine simplicity... which made him go and do the thing while she and Peter frittered their time away bickering." Richard is adored by Clarissa as he is more active, caring, and involved with society. Conversely, Peter is seen to waste his time and is unproductive which influences Clarissa when they are together frittering their time away. Woolf positions the reader to question the importance of emotional sensitivity and traditional work to the development of a meaningful life.

Clarissa decides that she will invite Ellie and is suddenly overcome by sadness. She attempts to trace the cause of her sudden sadness with meticulous examination "as a person who has dropped some grain of pearl or diamond into the grass and parts the tall blades very carefully." The imagery reflects the value of happiness and the constant effort that is needed to maintain it and overcome feelings of depression and hopelessness. Clarissa concludes that it must be caused by the way both Richard and Peter criticise the way she views her parties. Their criticism affects Clarissa, reflecting her insecurity and desire to be **venerated**.

Venerated: to be viewed with great respect, reverence, and admiration.

Richard is concerned about Clarissa's excitement due to her prior heart trouble, and Peter thinks she is snobbish and desires the company of influential people. To Clarissa, however, "both were quite wrong. What she liked was simply life." Clarissa's parties offer her a chance to escape and be excited about something; **fleeting** break from the **ritualistic** and mundane life she leads. Her parties provide Clarissa with a sense of purpose and reason to endure her illness and suffering.

Fleeting: something brief and short-lasting.

Ritualistic: to be performed in the same way with no variation.

Clarissa perceives her parties as a gift and a way of bringing people together. She likes to feel like she provides an important service to others as "an offering; to combine, to create; but to whom?" Clarissa's self-confidence is eroded by the criticisms of Richard and Peter as she sometimes struggles to see her value in the world. This makes Clarissa's happiness **precarious** and dependent on others. Despite Clarissa believing her parties were about bringing people together, she actively excludes people and her parties remain limited to the upper echelon of society.

Precarious: not secure; unreliable or uncertain.

Section 9

Elizabeth enters Clarissa's room quietly, trying not to disturb Clarissa as she rests. Clarissa has only recently recovered from her illness. The door remains ajar as Miss Kilman remains on the other side attempting to listen in. Miss Kilman wears a **mackintosh** and "degradingly poor." Clarissa is quite rude and **condescending** towards her as she comes from the "most worthless of all classes – the rich, with a smattering of culture."

Mackintosh: a rubber raincoat.

Condescend: to demean with an attitude of superiority.

Miss Kilman is exhausted and despises Clarissa. She has never been happy in London, and she only endures the **animosity** between her and Clarissa because she has no other options for work. Miss Kilman is German and is proud of her heritage. Before the war, she was given a chance to work at Miss Dolby's school. However, she was promptly dismissed when the war began as "she would not pretend that the Germans were all villains." Great Britain had entered the war to fight against German invasion of Western Europe. This naturally led to defensive anti-German sentiments at the time which caused distrust, scepticism, and fear of German people living in Great Britain.

Animosity: strong hostility and friction.

Miss Kilman's refusal to condemn Germans reflects the strength of her beliefs and her seclusion from British society. The **insular** society discriminated against Miss Kilman and Germans with no consideration of their humanity. Miss Kilman's only days of happiness were in Germany, leading to her becoming particularly bitter, dejected, and resentful. Miss Kilman was **enthralled** by history and enjoyed learning about it. Richard met Miss Kilman and allowed her to teach Elizabeth history. Miss Kilman also gives life lessons to Elizabeth which has put her at odds with Clarissa as their values and perspectives clash.

Insular: ignorant and lacking an understanding beyond one's own experiences.

Enthralled: captivated or fascinated by something.

Miss Kilman had converted to Christianity two years prior. She had attended a church where her "bitter and burning" feelings and rage had been alleviated. As she listened to Reverend Whittaker, "the hot and turbulent feelings which boiled and surged in her had been **assuaged**." Religion offers Miss Kilman the chance to view the world as more purposeful and ordered, allowing her to cope and deal with the vast injustice and abject cruelty of the world.

Assuaged: to be put at ease or to make a feeling less intense.

Since converting to Christianity, Miss Kilman found that she no longer envies Clarissa. She attempts to subdue her bitterness as much as she can, but her fury persists. Miss Kilman is angered by Clarissa's privileges and believes she and other aristocratic women "should have been in a factory." Miss Kilman finds pleasure in imagining Clarissa as less wealthy and protected from adversity, reflecting her deep-seated angst and resentment that has developed. She finds satisfaction from imagining others suffering and having to endure factory work. Miss Kilman is emblematic of the toxic power of envy to consume individuals and undermine their compassion, empathy, and desires for self-improvement.

Elizabeth goes upstairs, claiming to have forgotten her gloves. She leaves because she doesn't want to be in the same room as Clarissa and Miss Kilman. Elizabeth believes they hate each other and finds their relationship numbing. Miss Kilman declares Clarissa to be a "fool!" and a "simpleton!" who has "have trifled [her] life away! And there rose in [Miss Kilman] an overmastering desire to overcome her; to unmask her." This highlights Miss Kilman's **spite** and hatred that has consumed her.

Miss Kilman is dissatisfied with her life and channels her contempt onto Clarissa. She wishes she could "make her weep; could ruin her; humiliate her; bring her to her knees crying." We see that her anger is destructive and contributes to her unhappiness. Miss Kilman has a sense of **righteousness** and moral superiority over Clarissa which makes her feel calm and distracts her from her suffering.

Clarissa sees through Miss Kilman's religious exterior and detects the **malice** this conceals. Clarissa believes that she is destroying Elizabeth and trying to steal her. Miss Kilman says that she is going to take Elizabeth to the stores. Miss Kilman's image and façade seemed to crumble in the presence of Clarissa. Miss Kilman "lost her **malignity**, her size, became second by second merely Miss Kilman." This contrasts Miss Kilman to Clarissa as Clarissa seems more powerful due to her status and wealth. But Miss Kilman and Clarissa are united in the personal suffering they face as they struggle with their identity, sense of self and finding meaning.

Clarissa laughs as she sees "the dwindling of the monster." This monster is Miss Kilman's power which **dissipates** in the presence of Clarissa. Elizabeth returns to the room and they leave. Clarissa reminds Elizabeth about her party that night. Clarissa watches a neighbouring woman through the window as Elizabeth and Miss Kilman leave. The neighbour climbs upstairs and parts the curtains to her bedroom. Clarissa finds peace in watching the old woman who is unaware of Clarissa watching her. This reminds Clarissa of "the privacy of the soul," and to Clarissa, this privacy is threatened by Miss Kilman and the power religion has.

Spite: a desire to hurt, annoy, or offend someone.

Righteousness: moral goodness and a belief in one's own sense of justice.

Malice: ill will or extreme hostility.

Malignity: evil and dangerous.

Dissipate: disappear, vanish, or disperse.

There is a similar threat by Sir William who abuses his authority to dominate and convert others, stripping their humanity and forcing conformity. Clarissa now thinks of Peter again and how love can be destructive. She believes love makes him selfish and bitter. The clocks of Big Ben strike which reminds Clarissa that she has to call Ellie Henderson to invite her to the party.

The story shifts now to Miss Kilman and Elizabeth who are walking outside as they hear the clock striking. Miss Kilman is disturbed by Clarissa's laughter and how it elicited "the **fleshly** desires" that she has been trying to subdue. Miss Kilman is upset that she does not have the wealth like Clarissa to buy pretty clothes or make herself better. She thinks Clarissa has it easy and is **sombre** because she has been denied these pleasures and luxuries.

Fleshly: relating to carnal human desire and bodily pleasure.

Sombre: deep and intense sadness.

This bitterness leaves Miss Kilman dissatisfied and angry. Reverend Whittaker had **consoled** Miss Kilman and encouraged her to believe that she has a purpose in life. He argued that pain and suffering are not for nothing, but part of a journey towards happiness and peace. Reverend Whittaker said that God understands her agony, but Miss Kilman questions the injustice of the world, "why should she have to suffer when other women, like Clarissa Dalloway, escaped?" The contrast between Miss Kilman and Clarissa exposes how nobody is immune to feelings of inadequacy.

Console: to offer comfort in the midst of grief or disappointment.

Miss Kilman's conflict with Clarissa emphasises her discomfort with their inherent imbalance. To Miss Kilman, Clarissa has had an easy life whereas she has suffered from discrimination, poverty, and isolation, so is now left deeply unhappy. Miss Kilman attempts to suppress her envy and masks it with a sense of moral superiority over Clarissa. This is a much more comforting thought than the realisation of one's inadequacy and inferiority.

Miss Kilman enjoys eating, one of the few things she finds joy from. Her only other source of joy in London is her experiences with Elizabeth. Miss Kilman speaks **candidly** with Elizabeth and describes her distress as "like a wheel without a tyre... jolted by every pebble." The simile represents how isolated and hopeless she is as every minor problem is amplified. Miss Kilman lives in a state of dread, trudging along with little hope of escape.

Candidly: honestly and with sincerity.

Miss Kilman had taught Elizabeth about the war and encouraged her to consider other points of view. She had taken Elizabeth to church and gave her books about law, medicine, and politics. Miss Kilman and Elizabeth enter a store where they have tea together. Miss Kilman encourages Elizabeth to **ardently** pursue her passions, believing that modern society no longer inhibits women of her generation from working in any profession.

Ardently: with great passion and enthusiasm.

Miss Kilman believes that "her career was absolutely ruined" but Elizabeth's generation has the chance to live a life with more control and independence. This reflects the changing attitudes towards women and the hope that women would no longer be limited to passive roles.

Miss Kilman has hope that the next generation of women can be active members within society. Such advancements for women included the right to vote and increased participation in employment due to the mobilisation of war.

Elizabeth lives a very sheltered life with little consideration of the struggles of impoverished people. It was only through Miss Kilman that Elizabeth became more exposed to the challenges of life and the incredible suffering that many people face each day. As Elizabeth finishes her tea, she wants to leave but Miss Kilman convinces her to stay some more. Miss Kilman's attachment to Elizabeth reflects her desperation to feel loved, appreciated and wanted.

Extremely unhappy and battling her feelings of rage, Miss Kilman lives **vicariously** through Elizabeth. Her only joy comes from food and Elizabeth, and she hopes that Elizabeth will have the opportunities that society had denied her. Miss Kilman attempts to subtly dissuade Elizabeth from attending Clarissa's party as she does not want the "parties [to] absorb her" like they absorbed Clarissa. Miss Kilman enjoys spending time with Elizabeth but fears that her depressing state makes Elizabeth bored, disinterested, and maybe even repulsed by her.

Vicariously: to derive pleasure and experiences through the actions of another person.

Miss Kilman is desperate to keep the conversation going and says that she is never invited to parties and declares "I'm plain, I'm unhappy." Elizabeth is unsure of how to respond. She remains silent "like some dumb creature who has been brought up to a gate for an unknown purpose, and stands there longing to gallop away." This reflects Elizabeth's lack of independence and her unease with Miss Kilman's confessions. Elizabeth is disturbed by the way Miss Kilman talks. Miss Kilman is consumed by bitterness, despair, and resentment.

Elizabeth goes to pay and leaves Miss Kilman alone. Miss Kilman is devastated as Elizabeth leaves and is overwhelmed by "shocks of suffering." She believes Clarissa has triumphed and succeeded in stealing Elizabeth from her. This is a dangerous perspective that views Elizabeth as a possession rather than an individual. Miss Kilman returns to her grim state and goes to pray in the Abbey (Westminster Abbey, an Anglican church). Prayer and religion is an attempt to suppress her feelings of inadequacy as she looks for escape from misery.

Elizabeth goes and waits for an omnibus. As she waits, people around her take notice of her fancy clothes. Elizabeth feels that this attention is a burden on her, and she much prefers time alone, especially out in the country. The country symbolises liberation to Elizabeth as people in the country do not notice her as much and there are no expectations for her to attend parties. She describes London as dreary and how she enjoys time in the country with her father and dogs.

Elizabeth gets on a random omnibus and sits up top with no care for where it goes. The movement of the omnibus empowers Elizabeth and she thinks of how she could be a doctor or a farmer. The omnibus delivers Elizabeth to the Strand (a street in a working class neighbourhood) where she is enticed by the notion of professions. She compares the people here with the upper class and believes that these people's minds are occupied with "thoughts of ships, of business, of law, of administration." These ambitions stimulate Elizabeth and give her hope that her future will be important and meaningful.

The omnibus is representative of Elizabeth's uncertainty about her future. Like the omnibus, Elizabeth moves through life with no clear goal or destination in mind. Instead, she is sheltered and consumed by trivial matters that she resents. The ambitions Elizabeth has remain frozen in her mind as she is unable to imagine herself pursuing these hopes. Elizabeth **relinquishes** herself to mediocrity and to the expectations that subdue her.

Relinquish: to give up or hand over control.

The joy Elizabeth gets from her aspirations is undercut by the realisation that "she must go home." Elizabeth chooses to return home for Clarissa's party which represents her resignation. This cements Elizabeth's role as Clarissa's possession, "my Elizabeth." Her aspirations for a life free from her burdens remains a **tantalising** dream. Elizabeth's hopes are tarnished and is symbolised through the omnibuses which have "suddenly lost their glow." The loss of light represents Elizabeth's abandonment of her ambitions and acceptance of mediocrity.

Tantalising: an exciting desire for something that is unattainable.

Section 10

We return to Septimus and Lucrezia who are at home. Septimus is watching the sunlight on the wallpaper as Lucrezia is making a hat for Mrs Peters. Mrs Peters is the daughter of Lucrezia's friend and neighbour, Mrs Filmer. Mrs Filmer was often frightened by Septimus when he would suffer from his delusions and Lucrezia wants to show her gratitude. Septimus has not improved and often gets Lucrezia to write down his ramblings and visions about war, Shakespeare, and his belief that there is no death. Septimus' mind is full of discoveries of the cruelty of human nature and truths of the world.

Lucrezia is distraught and has become irritated by Septimus. Lucrezia is afraid that there is nothing left of their marriage and that it is impossible for her to find happiness again. Septimus sees himself drowned, "lying on a cliff with gulls screaming over him." This emphasises his severe detachment from reality and offers little hope for peace from the visions that torment his mind and leading him to insanity. Septimus' illness appears to have changed him **irrevocably**, manifesting in the vast gulf between husband and wife that Clarissa reflects on. Their gulf overwhelms them and leaves them feeling lost, alone, and empty.

Irrevocably: something that cannot be undone, changed, or reversed.

At one point, Septimus momentarily returns to his normal self as "he began, very cautiously, to open his eyes." He looks around to confirm that all that he has seen and heard is really there and not part of his visions. Septimus' hesitance signifies the power his condition has over him. To his surprise, everything around him is real and nothing is moving. As he looks at Lucrezia, he keeps his eyes partially shut as he is afraid that she will appear deformed. Septimus gradually opens his eyes, fearful that this return to sanity will not last. He is pleased to see that everything looks perfectly normal. Septimus cannot understand why he has been acting so strange and irrational.

Septimus' visions, revelations and despair are "burnt out, for he had a sense" as he watches Lucrezia make the hat for Mrs Peters. This contrasts with the Septimus we have seen so far, and there is a sense of hope in his return to sanity. Septimus and Lucrezia are now able to talk and laugh together as normal. They mess around and have fun by making ridiculous hats, genuinely enjoying each other's company. Lucrezia is filled with incredible joy – "never had she felt so happy! Never in her life!"

Septimus designs the hat whilst Lucrezia sews it. Septimus' desperation for normality is seen through his belief that making the hat is his most significant accomplishment in life. Septimus has a sense of achievement and pride in designing the hat and this simple act **rejuvenates** his soul. He longs for a sense of purpose and stability. Septimus and Lucrezia dance and skip around the room with **zeal**. Septimus reads the paper as he begins to feel tired. Content and filled with joy, Septimus falls asleep.

Septimus awakes suddenly and finds himself "alone, exposed on this bleak **eminence**, stretched out." This represents his vulnerability and fear. Septimus calls out to Evans but hears no response. His visions are still absent from his mind. Septimus is **inundated** with insecurity and fear which leads him to believe that he will always be alone and suffering. He sees himself as being punished by the world for being incapable of feeling. Septimus' numbness inhibits growth, happiness, and intimacy.

Lucrezia returns and mentions that Mrs Filmer is no longer going to Brighton as planned. Lucrezia appears liberated as she makes the most of Septimus' return to normality. This energises Lucrezia and she reflects on how they met in Milan and how gentle he was. She has always admired the way Septimus would never get "wild or drunk" and how he protected her from his suffering in the war. Most of all, Lucrezia cherishes the way she can talk honestly with Septimus.

Septimus thinks back to the way Sir William had insisted that he must be separated from Lucrezia to rest. He questions, "what right has Bradshaw to say 'must' to me?" Lucrezia attempts to calm Septimus by explaining that this was because Septimus had made threats of suicide. She showed Septimus everything that he had made her write down.

Rejuvinate: to restore, renew, or give new energy to.

Zeal: enthusiasm or passion in pursuit of an objective.

Eminence: an elevated patch of ground.

Inundated: overwhelmed or flooded by.

Septimus wanted the drawings and writings destroyed so that Sir William could not use them as evidence to separate him and Lucrezia. She says that she finds some of the drawings and writings to be beautiful. Instead of destroying them, she ties up the papers and hides them. Her love and desire to remain with Septimus allows her to "mount the appalling staircase, laden with Holmes and Bradshaw." This depicts Dr Holmes and Sir William as obstacles and oppressive forces that subdue Septimus. It is through Lucrezia's love and commitment to Septimus that the two can conquer these obstacles, providing a sense of hope. They are desperate to preserve the rare moment of happiness they are experiencing.

Dr Holmes arrives to see Septimus but Lucrezia blocks him and refuses to let him up the staircase. The hope from their intimacy and passion is undercut as Dr Holmes pushes Lucrezia aside. This causes Septimus to panic and he becomes consumed by the need to escape the situation. He is trapped and forces to choose between committing suicide and relinquishing his soul. Septimus believes his only option is the "rather **melodramatic** business of opening the window and throwing himself out." The distant and unfeeling description emphasises how removed Septimus is from his humanity due to his condition and cruel treatment.

Melodramatic: over-the-top or exaggerated emotional drama.

Septimus hesitates because he does not want to kill himself. He waits until the last moment possible. When Dr Holmes makes it to the door, Septimus plunges out the window to his death. Dr Holmes cries "the coward!" He goes outside to see if Septimus is conscious and finds him impaled on a railing. Septimus' decision to jump out of the window is a desperate attempt to free himself from the shackles of control. He defies conformity and repression and actively takes control of his fate.

The motivations of Septimus' suicide are quite clear. As readers, we have intimate knowledge of Septimus' struggles, his desires, and his internal conflict. What is less clear is whether suicide can be justified or a valid form of expression. Septimus' suicide appears to be justified and is depicted as a valid way of breaking free from society's cruelty and alienation.

Dr Holmes does not want Lucrezia seeing the body so he keeps her inside. Lucrezia seems to understand the decision Septimus made. She views his suicide as his final act of communicating his torment with the world. Dr Holmes appears **deplorable** in the way he minimises the situation and tries to escape responsibility. Dr Holmes drugs Lucrezia to keep her relaxed, but this can also be interpreted as a way of making sure she does not blame him. Lucrezia had felt let down by Dr Holmes and could choose to accuse Dr Holmes of contributing to Septimus' suicide.

Deplorable: something unacceptable, shameful, or dishonourable.

Dr Holmes further attempts to free himself of responsibility as he speaks to Mrs Filmer. He acts **incredulous** and tells Mrs Filmer that no one is to blame, remarking "who could have foretold it?" The rhetorical question emphasises Dr Holmes' lack of sympathy and the woefully inadequate treatment Septimus received. Dr Holmes was never interested in rehabilitating Septimus and now seeks to shift responsibility rather than reconsider his approach to his patients. This juxtaposes the empathetic and caring expectations of doctors and further highlights the lack of understanding of mental health at the time.

Incredulous: unwilling to believe or accept something as true.

The striking of the clock returns as Lucrezia falls asleep. She is remembering the fond memories with Septimus and the joy they had experiences. Dr Holmes advises Lucrezia to not see the body because of how mangled it is. Septimus' suicide and Dr Holmes' apathetic nature exposes the cruelty of society that fails to support and engage with those suffering. This presents a grim view of the world where tragedy and loss seem inevitable.

Section 11

This story shifts to Peter who hears the bell of an ambulance. This is likely the ambulance that has collected Septimus' body. Peter is astonished at the way people instinctively moved to the side and let it pass without hesitation. He characterises civilisation as this "efficiency, the organisation, the communal spirit of London." The respect Peter has for civilisation and its institutions is undermined by the neglect of Septimus which contributed to his suicide.

Peter believes that the one's privacy is a privilege, an important place to express emotions and deal with suffering. Peter feels that his inability to deal with his pain in solitude and to weep is what has left him so isolated and vulnerable to Clarissa. Peter's discontent is due to not properly dealing with his emotions, instead succumbing to passion, fantasies and nostalgia. This leaves him in a perpetual struggle of identity.

Peter reflects on his friendship with Clarissa and how they would explore London together when they were young. Peter finds fulfilment through the intimate connections he makes with other people. Clarissa believes that the "unseen part of us" involves the places people go and who surrounds them. This can be combined to understand a person's identity. In this way, Peter's move to India represents his desire to suppress his feelings for Clarissa after rejection. He wanted to escape her alluring nature, and his return represents the impossibility to Peter's attempts to subdue his feelings.

Peter arrives at his hotel where some letters have been left for him. One letter is from Clarissa which annoys him "like a nudge in the ribs". Clarissa's presence is seen to be taunting and discomforting to Peter as he cannot stand the influence Clarissa has on his life. Peter is frustrated that he is unable to reconcile his feeling and move on, which is exacerbated by Clarissa's letter. To Peter, a letter is impersonal, insincere, and unfeeling. This contrasts the intimacy and genuine communication they once shared.

Peter hopes that Clarissa regrets her rejection of him. He thinks Clarissa was energised when she saw him and that she is bored with her mundane, conventional and mediocre life. Peter imagines her becoming overwhelmed with regret and sorrow after he left. Now, Peter is determined to not give in and read the letter. He thinks about the effort that Clarissa must have gone through to get this letter to him in the few hours since their meeting. Peter empties his pockets and his pocket-knife comes out "so naturally; so much more naturally than Clarissa." Through this use of juxtaposition, Woolf highlights Peter's **ambivalence**. Pocket-knives are predictable and rhythmic, but Clarissa is complex, confusing, and reserved.

Ambivalence: having mixed feelings or contradictory impressions about something.

Along with the pocket-knife Peter pulls out an image of Daisy in all white. He is torn between his feelings and fantasies. Peter thinks that Daisy may not agree to marry him after all. He knows that she must consider her two children and their age difference. Daisy is 24 years old and their time apart gives her the opportunity to reconsider their relationship and future. Peter wants to believe that he has moved on from Clarissa and loves Daisy entirely, but we see his internal conflict and uncertainty about his identity.

Peter's age prompts this self-reflection as he questions his worth and what he has left in him. He wonders if Daisy would be happier and better off with Peter gone so that she could remember him fondly rather than become disinterested later. This reflects the self-doubt that has become ingrained in Peter as he feels inadequate and lost, seeing himself as lacking purpose. He believes that if Daisy moves to London, he will simply "haunt and hover" rather than experience the vitality of life.

Despondent: to have lost hope or courage.

Peter is **despondent** as "Clarissa had sapped something in him permanently." This depicts Peter as incomplete and suggests that happiness is unattainable for him. Peter decides that he will go to Clarissa's party. He reasons to himself that he is only going so that he can ask Richard about what the British government is doing in India. We are aware that he is mostly going to see Clarissa again who he finds irresistible.

Summer time: daylight savings time where clocks are put forward one hour in the summer.

It is evening and Peter observes that, for some people, the day is only just beginning. He finds "Mr. Willett's **summer time**" inspiring and a reflection of the vast changes to English society whilst he was away. Peter notices how joyful the youth seem to be as they can capture the evening, harnessing it and finding hope from it. The hope and freedom of youth contrasts Peter's bleak and insipid state of mind.

As Peter walks through the streets of London to Clarissa's party, he envies the energy of the youth and the way they act unbothered and unconcerned. They live in the moment, free from the uncertainty that plagues Peter.

Peter is enthralled by the significant changes to society, "that shift in the whole pyramidal accumulation which in his youth had seemed immovable". This symbolises the changing social order that fascinated Peter, especially the weakening of the ruling class aristocrats, a reorientation of priorities post the destruction of World War I, and some loosening of the oppression of women.

Peter sees people out enjoying life and embracing each other "as if the whole of London were embarking in little boats... as if the whole place were floating off in carnival." This represents the purity of human desires for joy and connection. Society is seen as harmonious and unified, yet Peter remains as an outsider, isolated from the experiences he craves. This is clear as Peter feels like an imposition, "as if in the presence of some sacred ceremony." Peter is ultimately a lonely figure unsure of who he is and where he wants to go. He arrives at Clarissa's party where "the soul must brave itself to endure." This symbolises Peter's disdain for the superficiality of Clarissa's parties along with the inevitable pain he experiences when thinking about Clarissa, his regrets, and missed opportunities.

Section 12

Inside Clarissa's party, rumours are floating around that the Prime Minister will be in attendance. Yet "did it matter, did it matter in the least, one Prime Minister more or less?" This repetition illustrates the disinterest in the Prime Minister who symbolises tradition and authority, thereby conveying the decline of traditional institutions and their power within society. The Prime Minister is stripped of his value and is viewed as insignificant and has no purpose or importance beyond his title.

The ladies have gone upstairs to get ready whilst the men stayed downstairs, drinking and laughing in the dining room. Lucy notes that Elizabeth looks lovely in her pink dress and Elizabeth is wearing the necklace Richard had bought for her. This shows Elizabeth's acceptance of her role and fate as part of the upper class. The men join the women upstairs. Clarissa remains downstairs to greet guests as they arrive.

The men go upstairs where the women are as Clarissa continues to greet guests. Peter is quite critical of Clarissa's parties. Peter sees through Clarissa's façade and he views the way that Clarissa welcomes her guests with delight as "**effusive**, insincere." Peter knows no one at the party, opting to remain by himself; he feels out of place and regrets coming.

Effusive: to express gratitude with great enthusiasm.

Peter's criticism of Clarissa immediately affects her. Clarissa sees Peter watching and judging everything about her. This undercuts Clarissa's confidence as "he made her see herself," exposing the emptiness that lies within. Clarissa feels "quite sick to know that it was all going wrong, all falling flat." She feels that her party is underwhelming and lacks value now that she has seen Peter's disapproval.

Clarissa is annoyed by the way Peter critiques her yet is never willing to take risks and put himself out there. Clarissa questions, "why always take, never give?" This leads Clarissa to reflect on her party and sense of purpose. She remains **adamant** that it is more worthwhile to live an exciting and eventful life rather than remain inactive and "wandering aimlessly" in the background like Ellie Henderson.

Adamant: to be firm and unyielding in one's beliefs.

Ellie is excited to attend the party and Clarissa had reluctantly offered a last-minute invitation. Ellie can tell that Clarissa did not want to invite her. Clarissa and Ellie are cousins who have known each other all their lives and had spent time together at Bourton. However, over the years they had grown more distant and are now part of different worlds. To Clarissa, parties and prestigious events are common, but to Ellie they are rare and exciting.

Ellie is captivated by the extravagance of Clarissa's party and is thrilled to see Elizabeth. She stands alone, taking in the scene and the upper class guests that intrigue her. Ellie is content standing by herself, but Richard does not let her. They speak briefly before Peter interrupts to speak with Richard. A random curtain blowing out causes Clarissa to feel that her party is alive and has started. This helps to reassure Clarissa but she remains anxious and uneasy.

Clarissa is unable to enjoy herself as she questions her role as the party's host. She feels insignificant and believes "anybody could do it." This highlights how precarious Clarissa's sense of self is. She becomes so absorbed with the pursuing perfection and upholding conventions that she lacks identity. This is furthered when Clarissa is too preoccupied with ensuring everything is perfect that "she had quite forgotten what she looked like." Clarissa's sense of self is distorted by her insecurity and need to please.

Suddenly, Sally appears unexpectedly. This is the first time that we witness Sally in the present – everything that we have learnt about her thus far has come from the recollections of characters like Clarissa and Peter. Sally is introduced as Lady Rosseter which immediately suggests that Sally has morphed into an entirely new person. She is no longer the daring rebel of Bourton, but a mother consumed by **orthodoxy**.

Orthodoxy: adherence to conventions and traditions.

Sally's arrival shocks Clarissa. Sally is no longer the person Clarissa recognises. Clarissa appears mournful that "the **lustre** had gone out of" Sally. Clarissa notes that Sally seems to be "older, happier, less lovely." Sally is quick to talk about her "five enormous boys" and seems unrecognisable to the Sally depicted by Clarissa and Peter.

Lustre: an admirable or unique quality of a person; one's shine.

Before Clarissa and Sally can talk too much, the arrival of the Prime Minister is announced. Ellie is overwhelmed with excitement in the presence of the Prime Minister. Yet to others, the Prime Minister is dreadfully ordinary with nothing special about him. He is seen to have no power or significance.

The Prime Minister goes around to each of the guests, making polite conversation as "he tried to look somebody." It is an anticlimactic arrival that undermines the significance of the Prime Minister. This shows that he is out of touch and lacks authority and respect.

Everyone in attendance seems to have the same recognition as "they all knew, felt to the marrow of their bones, this majesty passing; this symbol of what they all stood for, English society." The Prime Minister is merely a symbol for English society. His fading significance signifies the fading relevance of traditions in 1920s society. This foreshadows a new era for England with an emphasis on hope and prosperity for all, not just the wealthy elites. This links to the historical context which saw English society transform post World War I with the development of the middle class, industrialisation, democracy, advancements in women's equality, and the decline of traditional institutions.

Peter is repulsed by the interactions the Prime Minister has and views the collection of aristocrats to be the "snobbery of the English." Peter is critical of Hugh and believes he is deeply insincere, lacking substance and genuineness. Peter shows disdain towards the guests at Clarissa's party, believing himself to be superior to them. This belief reinforces his status as an outsider as he refuses to **succumb** to conventions.

Succumb: to give in to pressure or temptation.

The Prime Minister goes around to introduce himself to each guest. Clarissa escorts him, "prancing, sparkling, with the stateliness of her grey hair." Clarissa's energetic movement is contrasted by her grey hair. This contrast between youth and old age reflects how Clarissa clutches to conventions as a way of finding security and predictability. This is Clarissa's defining nature and is a shift from her youthful self, emphasised as "age had brushed her." Clarissa is perpetually looking for reassurance that her life has meaning and value. Clarissa's age and Sally's abrupt reappearance forces her to contemplate whether the life she has built is worth all that she has sacrificed.

Clarissa is happy that the Prime Minister has attended the party. She is pleased that Sally, Peter and Richard can see and envy her. Clarissa feels the "intoxication of the moment", a sensation that overwhelms her and causes "**dilatation** of the nerves of the heart itself till it seemed to quiver." Clarissa cares immensely about her reputation and uses her parties and the Prime Minister's prestige to portray herself as successful.

Dilatation: expansion or widening.

Clarissa cares greatly about her perception, especially Peter's, and desires to be adored and respected with the status of the upper class. Yet her actions have "a hollowness" that erodes her confidence, and she now realises that "they satisfied her no longer as they used." This creates a sense of unease about Clarissa's identity, underlining its fragility. There is only so long that Clarissa can maintain the façade and suppress her instincts.

The Prime Minister departs, leaving Clarissa to dwell on Peter's criticism. His stare seems to have affected Clarissa and she now views her party with his **cynicism**. Clarissa, now absorbed by her party, moves between the many guests to entertain them. She is determined to make sure they are enjoying her party, or at least appear to be enjoying it.

Cynicism: the jaded belief that people are only motivated by self-interest.

Clarissa moves between groups of people throughout the night and we are given many names of the aristocratic guests. These are well-renowned people of nobility and power. Clarissa never stays engaged in conversation long. She feels it is her duty to get to every guest, emphasised as she "must" move on quickly each time she begins a new conversation. This reflects her insecurity as she feels that she must justify her existence and the party to each guest. This is seen as she professes "I had hoped to have dancing", cementing Clarissa's persistence for everything to be perfect. All of this contributes to Clarissa's superficiality which dominates her present nature.

Aunt Helena arrives and is depicted as old and frail. She is over 80 years old and uses a stick to help walk upstairs. Aunt Helena is an archaic symbol of the past as she is attached to memories of orchids, which she had studied whilst travelling in India in the 1860s. Clarissa and Peter have not spoken yet, but Clarissa summons Peter to talk with Aunt Helena about his time in India. Aunt Helena enjoys being able to talk to Peter about orchids and Burma as he listens intently to her.

Clarissa is quick to move on to Lady Bruton next. She likes Clarissa and admires her qualities, although they have little in common. Lady Bruton always struggles to make conversations with Clarissa, and she views Clarissa's charm as a hindrance to Richard for "he had lost his chance of the **Cabinet**." Lady Bruton believes that Clarissa's self-interest means she is unable to support Richard's career. Clarissa and Lady Bruton's brief, superficial interaction reflects the shallowness of their characters and the prioritisation of status and materialism over genuine connection.

Cabinet: senior members of the government who collectively make important decisions.

Lady Bruton is eager to speak with Peter and hear his opinions. Lady Bruton is restless and feels that she has been robbed in her life. At her old age, she laments that she never had the opportunities to lead others and be a general like her ancestor was. Lady Bruton's dreams, intelligence, and potential are "**debarred** by her sex." Lady Bruton represents the stifling of women of the time, even those among the upper class, as they were largely excluded from the public sphere. What Lady Bruton dreams of being was not seen as appropriate or fit for a woman. Lady Bruton suffers a similar kind of unnerving pain and an identity crisis as Clarissa does – they are not outliers. Sally tries to engage in conversation with Clarissa, but she is too preoccupied with entertaining her guests. Clarissa asks Sally and Peter to stay so that they can all chat once everyone else has left.

Debarred: excluded, prohibited, or disqualified from.

Sally and Peter are reminiscing on the past as Clarissa notes Sally's "voice was wrung of its old ravishing richness; her eyes not aglow as they used to be." Sally's transition into a conventionally respectable woman has stripped her of her individuality and the uniqueness that captivated Clarissa. Sally has lost her daring nature, the recklessness that Clarissa used to believe would "end in some awful tragedy; her death; her **martyrdom**." The excitement and thrill of Sally's youth is contrasted with her present mundanity as "she had married, quite unexpectedly, a bald man with a large buttonhole." The blunt, dull descriptions of her ordinary husband evoke a sense of disappointment. This criticism of Sally suggests that it is far more important to pursue personal satisfaction and individuality rather than conventionality.

Martyrdom: dying for a cause one strongly believes in.

Clarissa's thoughts about Sally and Peter are interrupted by the return of her need to be the perfect hostess. This compelling force means "she must leave them" as Sir William Bradshaw and Lady Bradshaw arrive late to the party. Sir William immediately goes to speak with Richard about a parliamentary bill he wants to pass through the **House of Commons**.

House of Commons: the lower house of British parliament where elected representatives debate and vote on legislation.

As Richard and Sir William discuss the bill, Clarissa tries to pinpoint why exactly she dislikes Sir William. Clarissa remembers how one time she had sought his advice and, whilst she believed he gave reasonable advice, Clarissa was relieved to get away from him. Clarissa remembers how she saw a "poor wretch sobbing" in the waiting room but can not identify specifically what about Sir William troubles her. Richard agrees with Clarissa as he "didn't like [Sir William's] taste, didn't like his smell." They acknowledge Sir William's skill, so their unsettling feeling about him highlights his unsympathetic nature.

Clarissa overhears Sir William talking about the "**deferred** effects of shell shock." At the same time, Lady Bradshaw explains to Clarissa that they were late because Sir William was informed of a young man who had killed himself. The young man used to be in the army and is Septimus, although Clarissa does not know who Septimus is and has no relation to him. This is the case that Sir William raises with Richard.

Deferred: postponed until later.

The talk of a young man's suicide greatly disturbs Clarissa. She initially appears only to be concerned with her party, outraged that the Bradshaws have the audacity to bring talk of death to her party. Distraught, Clarissa goes to be alone in the room where Lady Bruton and the Prime Minister had earlier gone to speak. She thinks that someone may be in there, "but there was nobody... There was nobody." The repetition reinforces Clarissa's isolation and the fear she experiences in her old age.

The talk of death was an invasion to Clarissa's party as the "party's splendour fell to the floor." It threatened her reputation as the perfect hostess. Clarissa considers the man's action and struggles to understand what could motivate someone to take their life. Clarissa faces an existential crisis as she feels pressured to return to the crowded rooms where "people kept on coming."

Transfixed: unable to move due to fear or astonishment.

Defiance: bold resistance or disobedience.

Clarissa remains perplexed and **transfixed** by the thought of the man's suicide. She realises that "death was **defiance**. Death was an attempt to communicate" with a world that readily abandons and represses those who do not fit neatly into society's traditions. Clarissa views Septimus' suicide as a pure, uninhibited act of expression. She admires the sense of authentic communication, the boldness to take control of their life. Clarissa acknowledges "there was an embrace in death" as death offers a chance to dictate one's fate, to escape a horrific life of isolation and despair.

Clarissa questions, "had he plunged holding his treasure?" Treasure is metaphorical of the soul, a person's conviction and dignity. Clarissa considers the possibility that suicide gives a chance for someone to preserve their soul and resist the repression and enforced conformity that permeates society. Clarissa reflects on the happiness she felt with Sally as she remembers when she declared "if it were now to die, 'twere now to be most happy." Clarissa feels detached from her former self where she had ambitions for autonomy, excitement, and **flair**.

Flair: uniqueness, creativity, and stylishness.

This new perspective contrasts Clarissa's fear of old age and death as it constricts her and reminds Clarissa of her unfulfilled ambitions. Clarissa imagines that Septimus was a victim of the oppressive force of Sir William. The thought of Sir William causes "the terror; the overwhelming incapacity" that Clarissa experiences to return. Her insecurity and existential dread are deep-seated "in the depths of her heart," something that must be grappled with to avoid succumbing to fear. Clarissa's hope for a more fulfilling life is through becoming more decisive and truer to her innate desires.

Clarissa reflects on the simplicity of Bourton and the overwhelming joy she felt there. It remains a pure memory untainted by the pressures of conformity and conventionality. Clarissa goes to the window and sees the same old woman from before. The woman is now preparing for bed. Clarissa is entranced by her mundane actions as she moves around the room and pulls down the blind. The striking of the clocks returns, intensifying the moment and signifying an end to Clarissa's self-interrogation.

As the clocks strike, Clarissa is forced back to reality, and she imagines that Septimus struggled like she has but believes that he maintained his soul's purity through suicide. Conversely, Clarissa has actively and intentionally abandoned her purity and sincerity for a conventional and safe life. Septimus' refusal to give in and surrender his identity cements to Clarissa the importance of being genuine, passionate, and true to oneself.

Anaphora: repetition of words or phrases at the start of sentences.

Clarissa knows that "she must go back. She must assemble. She must find Sally and Peter. And she came in from the little room." The truncated sentences and **anaphora** of 'she must' emphasises Clarissa's need to deal with her internal crisis. She returns to the party reinvigorated as Clarissa is now determined to reignite her passion and connection with Sally and Peter.

We return to Sally and Peter who are talking on the sofa. They are catching up and comparing their lives now to when they were younger. Peter reveals to Sally that he never ended up pursuing writing. We learn that Sally had very little money when she was young. To go to Bourton, she had to sell a ring passed down to her from her family that was bestowed on them by Marie Antoinette, the final queen of France before the French royal family was stripped of power in the French Revolution. The giving away of the ring symbolises how Sally lived for the moment and did not care about material possessions or tradition. This contrasts her present self as she now takes pride in her wealth, the status of her husband, their servants, and their conservatories.

Sally is astonished by the life Clarissa leads and her personality. It bewilders Sally as she feels Clarissa "lacked something" and believes that Peter understands it too. They are connected to Clarissa's childhood and know that she is vastly different to what she dreamt of becoming. Sally is also dismayed by Clarissa's choice to marry Richard as she wonders "how could Clarissa have done it?" Sally's surprise reinforces Clarissa's transition as she sacrificed her aspirations and flair for safety.

The consistent flashbacks to their youth as Peter and Sally converse reflect how they yearn for the freedom and openness they once had. The flashbacks underpin the fact that their ambitions and aspirations never amounted to anything. As a result, they are unhappy with their present existence and identity as their days are monotonous and consumed with superficiality. Sally and Peter speculate about Clarissa's nature as they have both drifted apart from Clarissa over the years. They wonder about the guests that surround them and Sally suggests that it is difficult to truly know other people. Peter argues that maturity allows a person to understand others by observing.

The party is coming to an end and people have been gradually leaving. Sally and Peter see Elizabeth approach Richard. Richard confesses to Elizabeth that he is proud of her. Despite not intending to say it, he was overcome by the love and pride he feels when he sees Elizabeth and knows "it was his daughter," much to Elizabeth's delight.

Sally gets up from the sofa to go and speak with Richard, believing that Richard has improved. Peter hesitates as his emotions overwhelm him. He questions, "what is this terror? what is this ecstasy... What is it that fills me with extraordinary excitement?" These conflicting feelings are due to his attachment to Clarissa. The concluding lines of the novel answer these questions: "It is Clarissa, [Peter] said. For there she was." Clarissa has entered the room and the true reunion can begin.

The ending of *Mrs Dalloway* is unclear and uncertain. It offers no conclusion to the character's struggles, their relationships, or their future. However, there is some hope as Sally "felt more deeply, more passionately, every year," Richard – who could not tell Clarissa he loved her – is openly proclaiming his pride and love for Elizabeth, Peter is filled with excitement at the thought of Clarissa rather than dread, and Clarissa seeks to reignite her passions.

Chapter 4

Character Analysis

Clarissa Dalloway

Clarissa Dalloway is the main character in *Mrs Dalloway*. Clarissa is 51 years old and a member of the upper class. She is married to Richard Dalloway and together they have one child, Elizabeth. Clarissa has planned a party for the night and has invited prominent members of high society. Through flashbacks and the commentary of other characters we come to understand how radically different Clarissa is to her past self. Clarissa's present identity is consumed by insecurity and a desire to craft a respectable status. Clarissa has experienced significant grief and loss in her life. Her sister and mother died when Clarissa was a child, but these events are not detailed or explored in the novel. This **omission** positions the reader to focus on Clarissa's identity and the impacts of her suffering.

Omission: the act of excluding or leaving something out.

Clarissa cares immensely about the way she is perceived by others. As a result, her life is defined by the unrelenting quest for admiration, status and nobility. This comes at a personal cost to Clarissa's happiness, confidence, and satisfaction with life. At times, Clarissa is miserable, lacks purpose, and is confused about her identity. Clarissa rigidly observes the conventions of upper class life, choosing to remain within the boundaries that stifle her aspirations and hope.

It appears as if Clarissa's only value is as "the perfect hostess," a label Peter gave her. This label had made Clarissa cry as it exposed her superficiality and hollowness. Clarissa's desire for admiration and status is ever-present in the novel. Our introduction to Clarissa is as she decides to get the flowers for the party herself. This is a convenient way for Clarissa to be seen by others – including her neighbour and an old friend – as a way of seeking gratification.

Despite the confident and tough exterior Clarissa presents, she is sensitive to suffering and the pressures placed on her. She is deeply insecure and unsure of herself. Clarissa has suffered from mental health issues, although the extent of this is not made clear in the novel. Clarissa quite successfully portrays a façade of strength and assuredness, with only people from her past able to pierce this façade. Clarissa's identity has become **inextricably** linked to her status as a hostess, as someone who pleases others and is revered. This is evident in the novel's title which places focus on her status as someone's husband rather than on her individuality.

Inextricably: unable to be separated or freed from.

Clarissa's insecurity has developed into a fear of sharing intimacy. She finds Peter's emotional and sensitive nature as a risk. Clarissa is frightened of exposing herself and sees a relationship with Peter as unthinkable and a dangerous surrender. This fear pushed Clarissa to choose Richard over Peter as a safer option. Yet, despite this, Clarissa is never truly relaxed, and she keeps her most serious thoughts and dreams to herself. The choice of Richard reflects the context where marriage was more traditional and not as motivated by passionate love and fulfilment.

Clarissa chose the safety and security of Richard yet the spirit that finds Peter enchanting remains within her and is impossible to suppress. Clarissa's marriage to Richard is mundane. He is a conservative politician with connections that allow Clarissa to be part of the upper class world that sustains her. Peter, Richard, and Sally were all close to Clarissa at Bourton. Clarissa's decision to reject Peter and marry Richard signals the beginning of her plunge into conventional living.

Clarissa has great admiration for the free-spirited nature of Sally and Peter, however, Clarissa feels that she is incapable of acting in the same way. She fears that she lacks the strength to defy expectations and seek the autonomy that she has always craved. In a world of uncertainty and confusion, Clarissa's marriage to Richard is a safe choice where Clarissa can live an ordinary, simple and secure life. Richard enables Clarissa to pursue her **insatiable** obsession with her reputation.

Insatiable: unable to be satisfied.

Clarissa's only purpose comes from her parties. When we see her as a hostess, she is consumed by anxiety as she feels obligated to ensure everything is perfect. Clarissa's relationship with Sally reveals a more carefree time where Clarissa actively pursued her emotions. Her constant reflection on Sally and their time together shows Clarissa's uncertainty as she is haunted by the thoughts of what could have been if she chose to favour her emotional interests over society's inflexible expectations.

Clarissa's love for Sally is seen to be authentic and pure; Sally invigorates Clarissa in a way that no man ever could. This passionate attachment to Sally stems from the deaths of Clarissa's mother and sister as a child. At the time the novel was written, lesbian relationships were highly **taboo**, yet Woolf wrote fondly of lesbian and intimate female relationships as a source of liberation and an act of rebellion against marriage. Marriage can be seen as a core structure of a patriarchal society and a catastrophe that Clarissa and Sally could escape from.

Taboo: something off-limits and prohibited by societal customs.

Clarissa values her privacy and cherishes it. She is fascinated with the old neighbourly woman that she watches. Clarissa has glimpses into her most intimate moments of solitude which reminds Clarissa of the privacy of the soul. When her party is invaded with the talk of death, Clarissa is outraged and stunned. Despite the overwhelming urge to maintain order and control of her party, Clarissa is confronted with the most extreme suffering. It is here where she seeks to change direction.

Clarissa seems to understand Septimus' suicide despite never knowing him. She acknowledges the power of taking control of one's fate and of resisting the pressures of society to conform. Clarissa genuinely loves the world of London that she is absorbed in. But Clarissa is sometimes struck with the sombreness that comes with the tantalising thoughts of how her life could be different if she had been more daring and courageous. The ending of the novel suggests that Clarissa has found the courage to rekindle her passions.

Septimus Warren Smith

Septimus Warren Smith is the main character of the novel's secondary plot. He does not know Clarissa, but they have significant parallels. Septimus is around thirty years old and is a veteran who fought in World War I. The horrific experiences he endured in the war have permanently scarred him and he has been unable to receive sufficient help from doctors. Septimus spends the day with his wife, Lucrezia Warren Smith, before killing himself to escape his life's suffering.

Septimus was eager to enlist to fight in World War I, being one of the first to volunteer. He was commended for his bravery and was seen as an outstanding solider. As a result, Septimus was quickly promoted. Septimus shared a close bond with his officer, Evans, who died during the war. The events of the war led to Septimus developing post-traumatic stress disorder (PTSD) which was severely misunderstood at the time.

Early in the novel, Septimus hears a car as the sound of a whip cracking. Whilst others are startled, Septimus is terrified as it triggers memories of the war, a common symptom of PTSD. Septimus' fears are too overpowering and chaotic. He is unable to maintain his sanity or control his hallucinations; the fearful sounds of war remain deeply embedded in his subconscious. Septimus also struggles to maintain traditional masculinity in a society that ridicules and dismisses those who display suffering and mental health issues. His deep suffering from the war is seen as a sign of weakness and a personal failing.

Psyche: the human mind or soul.

Septimus' PTSD causes him great mental anguish, affects his **psyche**, and has harmed his relationship with Lucrezia. Septimus found it difficult to return to normal life after the war ended. He experiences hallucinations, including seeing trees move and witnessing Evans. Septimus hears voices and constantly speaks of suicide. He is trapped in his private world due to his insanity.

These visions and delusions are often mundane but sometimes present themselves as messages from the gods. Septimus believes he is being personally targeted so that he can reveal the secrets of life to the world. He is desperate to communicate these messages to others but is effectively silenced and ignored. Even Lucrezia does not entertain his delusions, although she does find some of his mad drawings and writings to be beautiful.

Septimus and Lucrezia's relationship has been damaged by his struggles with mental health. Septimus is angered by the way Lucrezia dismisses him as they are not able to properly engage. This represents the overwhelming impact of Septimus' disorder and underlines the need for **rehabilitation**. Lucrezia is desperate to repair and reignite their relationship. She takes Septimus to see multiple specialists to help Septimus recover.

Rehabilitation: the process of restoring someone to normal health after injury or illness.

Septimus first sees Dr Holmes then Sir William Bradshaw. Both give inadequate diagnoses, failing to understand the legitimacy and severity of Septimus' illness. Dr Holmes is persistent in his diagnosis that nothing is wrong with Septimus. Dr Holmes suggests Septimus' illness is a result of cowardice and that he needs to take an interest in things beyond himself, such as playing cricket or attending a music hall. Sir William emphasises the importance of having a sense of proportion and orders Septimus to rest and be moved to a home in the country. The doctors stifle Septimus and believe that order is superior to rehabilitation with no sensitivity to the mind. Septimus is alienated from society and even Lucrezia as he struggles to communicate his pain and torment.

The poor treatment Septimus receives reflects how ill-equipped doctors were at the time given their minimal understanding of mental illness. Septimus is portrayed as a victim of a repressive society where conformity and order are prioritised at the expense of individuality and personal growth. Septimus' service in the war is admirable yet he is abandoned by his country. The appalling treatment he experiences exacerbates his trauma and fails to show basic dignity and humanity. Woolf's own experiences with society's dismissiveness of mental health are likely inspirations to Septimus' characterisation.

Septimus echoes the anguish Clarissa faces. They both – largely on their own – grapple with incredible suffering and struggle with mental illness. Septimus and Clarissa never meet, but are united in the societal pressures that affect their sanity and daily lives. For Septimus, there is some hope that he has the potential to overcome it all through the love and support of Lucrezia. We see a brief time where Septimus and Lucrezia return to normal and genuinely bond and experience the vitality of life in making a hat for Mrs Peters. It is a beautiful moment which centralises sincere relationships as cornerstones of humanity and sanity.

Septimus is despondent and fearful, preventing him from communicating authentically. His delusions and society's judgement torture him to the point of suicide, which is a desperate last resort of liberation and escape. For him, this is a defiant gesture that he believes gives meaning to his experiences and adequately communicates how profound his suffering was.

Peter Walsh

Peter Walsh is a childhood friend of Clarissa who is deeply in love with her and is despondent following her rejection of his marriage proposal. Peter has never been able to move on from Clarissa and his longing for her remains **steadfast**. He has spent some time living in India and has just returned to London. Peter meets with Clarissa during the day where he is very emotional. He then attends Clarissa's party, catching up with Sally and judging Clarissa's nature as a hostess.

Steadfast: firmly fixed in place and unchanging.

Peter has had limited success in his life. He never became a writer like he dreamt and now exists in a state of uncertainty and dread. Peter had met a girl in India, Daisy, and he intends on starting a new life with her. Daisy is married to a Major in the Indian Army and together they have two children. She is much younger than Peter and plans on divorcing her husband. Peter is in London to discuss with lawyers Daisy's divorce. But his return to London forces Peter to confront his past, his failed dreams, and his love for Clarissa that has never relented.

Peter is sensitive, emotional, and in touch with his feelings. He is constantly reflecting in his mind on the world, its structure, and who he is. When Peter meets with Clarissa and tells her about Daisy, he breaks down in tears. Peter is bothered by the way Clarissa appears to tease him. He is determined to ignore the letter she sends to him but gives in to her charm. Peter struggles to reconcile his past with his present and feels alienated from society.

Peter has no clear sense of identity and is contrasted to the changing society of London. Peter admires the progress and modernity of London society. He is particularly fond of the efficiency and organisation of people and ambulances as they work cooperatively. The changes Peter observes expose how **static** Peter's affection for Clarissa is. He has never been able to move on and this has crippled his life and dreams.

Static: to remain unchanged and in place, motionless.

Unlike Clarissa, Peter appears unbothered by the pursuit of reputation and status typical of the upper class. Peter is content as an adventurer and being in touch with his emotions. Peter is especially critical of Clarissa's parties which he views as **pretentious**, self-indulgent and driven by ego. Peter despises the way Clarissa's shallowness and how she desires to always be seen by others. The ending of the novel sees some hope that Peter may overcome his obsession with Clarissa that has held him back.

Pretentious: trying to appear more important and impressive than one actually is.

Richard Dalloway

Richard Dalloway is a conservative politician and part of the aristocratic society. He is married to Clarissa and wooed her over Peter. Richard is honourable, well-respected and kind. As a politician he cares about the community he serves and is supportive of Clarissa. Richard spends the day having a lunch party with Lady Bruton and Hugh Whitbread, and purchases flowers for Clarissa.

Richard is a very conventional figure. He is described as genuine, a good person of high moral character, though also unimaginative and dull. Richard is a safe choice for Clarissa and he allows Clarissa to live the lavish and elitist lifestyle she desires. Richard struggles to engage with and express his emotions. He wants to make sure Clarissa knows that he loves her, so he decides to buy her flowers. But when Richard goes to give Clarissa the flowers, he is unable to **articulate** his feelings, though Clarissa understands the gesture.

Articulate: to speak and express one's thoughts or emotions.

Richard is motivated by a sincere desire to help people and improve society. Whilst he ardently works towards this, Richard has no potential for growth in his career. He has never become a cabinet minister and receives no acknowledgement, appreciation, or respect for his work within parliament. This suggests that genuine efforts to help advance society is not something that is valued in a society ruled by an upper class that directly benefits from the preservation of order and tradition. Substantial change to this order threatens the positions and privileges of those in power, so people like Richard are left on the sidelines and are inhibited from making meaningful contributions.

At Clarissa's parties, Richard is a dutiful, generous husband, prioritising her needs over his own. When Sir William wants to talk with Richard at Clarissa's party about a proposed law in parliament, Richard is eager to talk. This reinforces his **benevolence** and authentic nature. Richard's conventional nature **subsided** when he was able to tell Elizabeth he loves her at the end of Clarissa's party. This offers a sense of hope that Richard can express his emotions and has the potential for individual growth.

Benevolence: well-meaning, kind, and having good intentions.

Sally Seton

Sally Seton is a childhood friend of Clarissa's. She is in her fifties and is now married with five children. Like Clarissa, Sally has changed significantly since her time at Bourton. She used to be extremely daring, **inquisitive**, and rebellious, but has transformed into a more conventional person. Her identity has been moulded and now more closely aligns with the traditions of the upper class. Sally and Clarissa had an intimate relationship at Bourton but are now both married and distant from each other. Sally arrives unexpectedly at Clarissa's party where she catches up with Peter and is excited by seeing Clarissa again.

Subside: to become less intense or severe.

Inquisitive: curious or asking lots of questions.

The Sally we see in flashbacks to Bourton conflicts with the social expectations of women at the time. Rather than remaining passive, obedient, and soft-spoken, Sally liked to test boundaries and was fiercely unafraid of people in power. She was provocative, adventurous, and free-spirited. This enchanting **aura** is what made Clarissa fall in love with Sally. This fondness has lasted throughout the decades which emphasises the importance of Sally's genuine personality. It is only sincere individuality that is remembered; conformity is forgotten and is uninspiring.

Aura: an atmosphere that surrounds a person.

Sally had **eccentric** views of the world and would fantasise about changing the world with Clarissa. They once dreamt of conquering the world together and reforming it to their image. They viewed the concept of marriage as stifling and as a catastrophe, an act of surrendering to a man. In contrast, their passion and aspirations are liberating. Sally also engaged in more radical ideas such as abolishing private property. Sally also despised people like Hugh Whitbread, describing him as detestable and representing everything that is wrong with the English middle class.

Eccentric: unconventional, strange, and odd.

The comments and beliefs of Sally reinforce her rebellious and strong nature, but over the years she has softened. She has joined the middle class that she used to staunchly oppose and believe lacked anything pure. Sally has also married and had five boys. She has attained the title Lady Rosseter, which is emblematic of the elitism she viewed to be superficial and alienating. Now in her fifties, Sally has adjusted to the realities of the world and is now ingrained in the upper class lifestyle.

Whilst Sally has undergone this transformation, she seems to have retained her identity and purity. At Clarissa's party, Sally still appears authentic and true to herself. This is especially seen through her conversation with Peter. Therefore, Sally represents the notion that it is possible to maintain one's individuality without conforming entirely to the repressive pressures of society.

Doris Kilman

Doris Kilman is an educated German woman in her forties who enjoys history. She tutors Clarissa's daughter Elizabeth in history and develops some influence over Elizabeth as they become close. She wears an old, green mackintosh coat that is rather unappealing which suggests that she is **aloof** from society's judgement of appearances. Miss Kilman has recently converted to Christianity and has suffered a great deal from society that has left her bitter and resentful. This is most clear in Miss Kilman's contempt for Clarissa who encapsulates the upper class.

Aloof: indifferent, disinterested, or distant.

Miss Kilman feels victimised by society. When World War I began, she was dismissed from her teaching position at a school because she did not believe that all Germans were villains, being of German ancestry herself. This attitude and her heritage led to her being **ostracised** and without employment, leaving her lonely and vulnerable.

Ostracised: alienated or excluded from.

Her **plight** has caused her to despise the ruling class and those who support it. This is evident in her hatred and disdain for Clarissa, though this hostility is somewhat of a mask for Miss Kilman's envy for Clarissa's ability to enjoy the privileges and opportunities that were denied to Miss Kilman.

Plight: a difficult circumstance or struggle.

However, Miss Kilman is unable to acknowledge the reality of her jealousy and discontent, not wanting to confront her own feelings of inferiority or shame. Her envy of Clarissa stems from a feeling of inadequacy that has developed through society's mistreatment and repression. It is more comfortable for Miss Kilman to rage against Clarissa than to accept that she herself is flawed.

Miss Kilman's contempt for Clarissa cause turbulence between them – their interactions are feisty, uneasy, and filled with derision. Religion helps Miss Kilman to cope with the rage and injustice she feels. Through Reverend Whittaker, Miss Kilman was introduced to the Christian faith and was **enamoured** by its teachings. She is inspired, reinvigorated, and seeks to influence and convert Elizabeth.

Enamoured: admiring or being in awe of something.

Like most people, Miss Kilman desires a purpose. Society has robbed Miss Kilman of her ancestral pride and teaching, but religion provides her with a new chance for a meaningful and peaceful life. Miss Kilman believes that God is able to relieve her of the suffering and rage she endures. But despite Miss Kilman's conversion, her rage remains. She weaponises her faith and uses it as a justification for her anger, believing that it is God's will to destroy Clarissa.

As a result of Miss Kilman's loneliness and isolation from her German heritage, she becomes attached to Elizabeth, living vicariously through the young woman. Consequently, she encourages Elizabeth to pursue opportunities that Miss Kilman never had due to the forces of the patriarchy. In particular, she discourages Elizabeth from following in Clarissa's footsteps, much to Clarissa's **chagrin** as she sees Miss Kilman as a source of indoctrination.

Chagrin: irritation or displeasure.

Miss Kilman's character therefore contrasts greatly with Clarissa. They are from the opposite social classes, and whilst Clarissa leads a rather privileged, conventional and stable life, Miss Kilman had to work tirelessly for what she has now. Despite these differences, Miss Kilman and Clarissa are united in the deep suffering they face from society. They are both facing despair, unhappiness, and anxiety. This suggests that all people are vulnerable to the repressive nature of society, and that giving in to conformity only **perpetuates** suffering.

Perpetuate: to make something continue endlessly.

Lucrezia Warren Smith

Lucrezia Warren Smith is the wife of Septimus, 24 years old, and from Milan, Italy. She met Septimus when he was a solider just after the war had ended. They fell in love quickly and Lucrezia moved to London with him. However, Septimus' PTSD looms over their relationship, leaving Lucrezia feeling confused and alone. She tries to get help from multiple doctors to heal Septimus but faces callous indifference and inadequate treatment. Lucrezia is loyally committed to Septimus and is there when he kills himself.

Septimus' mental illness has severely damaged his relationship with Lucrezia. Lucrezia often talks over Septimus and tries to hide his hallucinations from others. This is because Lucrezia is aware of the shame and embarrassment that insanity brings within society, so she attempts to minimise his illness. The judgement of society places an enormous burden on Lucrezia whose instincts are to 'fix' Septimus rather than engage with him.

Lucrezia's life has changed dramatically since marrying Septimus and moving to London. Lucrezia used to be energetic and enjoyed life with her family in Italy. In England, with an entirely different culture, she is extremely lonely. Lucrezia depends on Septimus for love and connection, so him being ostracised by society causes great distress and unhappiness for Lucrezia. She is isolated from her family and her miserable state is seen through her becoming thinner and the fact that her wedding ring no longer fits on her finger.

Despite her inability to deal with his condition, Lucrezia still is immensely fond of Septimus and finds some of his writings and drawings – products of his delusions – to be beautiful, hinting at her desire to seek hope amidst tragedy. She is also committed to finding doctors to treat Septimus but is disheartened by their consistent failure to address the complexity of his condition. Their dismissive and unfeeling attitude disturbs Lucrezia.

Elated: to be extremely happy, excited, and joyful.

By contrast, she is overwhelmed with joy in the fleeting moment where Septimus returns to his normal self. Lucrezia is **elated** as she and Septimus make a hat for Mrs Peters and skip around the room jubilantly. Though she has at times been distraught and irritated by Septimus, even pondering whether their marriage is hopeless, this moment helps her remember why they fell in love.

However, this is swiftly followed by Septimus' suicide which leaves Lucrezia alone. We do not know what is to come next for Lucrezia, but her life in London has been plagued with tragedy, suffering, and loss.

Dr Holmes

Dr Holmes is a general practitioner who Septimus sees to help with PTSD. Dr Holmes downplays the significance and seriousness of Septimus' condition. He believes that there is nothing wrong with Septimus and advises him to simply take an interest in things beyond himself and find a hobby. Dr Holmes says that playing cricket or going to a music hall are good methods of noticing real things and getting rid of Septimus' hallucinations – though this would have been more understandable to Woolf's audience at the time, as contemporary readers we can acknowledge how woefully inadequate such attitudes and suggestions are.

Dr Holmes' dismissal stems from his ultimately unsympathetic view of Septimus. He would visit the couple each day and attempt to force Septimus to be better without addressing the causes of his suffering. When Septimus refused to see Dr Holmes, he forced his way in and scolded Septimus for making Lucrezia stressed. When his methods are questioned, Dr Holmes brushes off concerns and refers Septimus and Lucrezia to Sir William Bradshaw.

On the day this novel takes place, Dr Holmes' visit interrupts the **tranquillity** of Septimus and Lucrezia's return to normality. Dr Holmes pushes his way past Lucrezia who is desperate to keep him away from Septimus. Dr Holmes' abhorrent nature makes him an intruder and a threat to Septimus. Septimus decides to jump out a window to his death to escape Dr Holmes. Dr Holmes keeps Lucrezia away from Septimus' body and drugs her. This appears to be a cold-hearted, selfish attempt to avoid blame and responsibility for Septimus' actions. Dr Holmes' callousness is further seen as he tells Mrs Filmer that no one can be blamed for Septimus' suicide.

Tranquility: a state of peace and inner calm.

Dr Holmes represents society's apathetic response to serious mental anguish. Along with countless others, Septimus suffered from what he witnessed in the war. Dr Holmes' dismissiveness reflects society's denial of the war's trauma. The war's impacts are significant and **reverberate** throughout society, with Woolf condemning this cruel and unjust treatment.

Reverberate: to have ongoing, widespread consequences, like a ripple effect.

Sir William Bradshaw

Sir William Bradshaw is a well-renowned psychiatrist who sees Septimus after a referral from Dr Holmes. Like Dr Holmes, Sir William reflects the uncaring and merciless nature of society, along with its ruthless undermining of the severity of mental health. Sir William is adamantly committed to maintaining order and achieving what he calls "proportion."

Sir William enjoys the power he wields and is a symbol of the corruption of the aristocrats. He sticks with traditional methods of dealing with patients and strictly enforces the agenda of those in power. This comes at the expense of his patients who fail to receive the personalised care they need to overcome adversity.

Sir William at least seems to notice that Septimus' condition is serious and not nothing. He is critical of general practitioners like Dr Holmes, whose work Sir William is constantly trying to fix. However, Sir William's confidence in his methods causes him to lack empathy and be dismissive of Septimus. Sir William has a rigid, methodical approach that he implements. This undermines his ability to connect with his patients, ultimately preventing the best outcomes, specialised treatment, and rehabilitation.

Sir William is quick to decide that Septimus needs plenty of rest out in the country. He makes this recommendation with no consultation with Septimus or Lucrezia and believes that they need to be separated whilst Septimus recovers. Sir William undermines the legitimacy of Septimus' condition by saying that everyone has impulses and experiences moments of sadness. The poor interaction leaves Lucrezia hopeless, reflecting the unsympathetic nature of Sir William.

Sir William has an exceedingly high reputation as a psychiatrist. He has been knighted for his work and community service. Sir William is deeply entrenched in the upper echelon of society. His actions, particularly through his diagnosis of Septimus, makes Sir William emblematic of the tendency of those in power to believe they have a greater sense of authority over others. Sir William is in a position of power and he exerts this on those who are weaker than him.

Repugnant: unacceptable, revolting, or distasteful.

Sir William is motivated by a desire to ensure England remains pure. Like those in power, Sir William views people like Septimus as **repugnant** and unfit for normal society. Sir William takes joy in the power he has and is enthralled by converting his patients to his views of proportion. To Sir William, proportion means conformity, order, and obedience. He attempts to cast away society's flaws and problems, alienating people like Septimus. Woolf is particularly critical of Sir William's oppression of individuality in the pursuit of maintain social order.

Hugh Whitbread

Vain: having excessive pride in one's appearance, achievements, and value.

Hugh Whitbread is a friend of Clarissa and has a job at court. He is married to the Honourable Evelyn Whitbread who is often quite ill. Hugh often buys gifts for Evelyn. Hugh is incredibly **vain** and superficial. He is typically seen to be over-dressed, pompous, and privileged. Hugh sees Clarissa in the park that morning, then has lunch with Richard Dalloway and Lady Bruton, the latter of whom he helps write a letter to a newspaper. After the lunch party, Hugh and Richard walk the streets of London where he shops for jewellery for Evelyn.

Hugh likes to believe that he has an important job in the court and is a man of great significance. However, others see Hugh as reduced to nothing more than a messenger constantly running errands for the court. This conflict reveals that Hugh is more concerned with his perception and self-belief that he is a man of importance. This provides Hugh with confidence, pride, and a sense of purpose.

Hugh helps Lady Bruton write a letter to the editor of the *Times*. Lady Bruton is thrilled with his letter and his command of language, but Richard finds his letter to be snobbish. Hugh contrasts Richard as Hugh is concerned solely with his appearance and reputation. He lacks ambition but boasts of his position in the court. Conversely, Richard is more sincere, humble and benevolent. Richard is motivated by a desire to serve his community.

Hugh is an embodiment of the 1900s English gentlemen **archetype**. This concept centred around being a well-educated, affluent, and sophisticated man – in other words, everything that Hugh aspires to. However, Hugh is **oblivious** to the way people like Richard, Sally and Peter see him as shallow and pretentious. Woolf criticises the gentlemen of England by portraying Hugh as consumed by the need to feel and appear important and special. He is the epitome of the upper class that clutches to their social status and the privileges they have inherited.

Archetype: a typical example or the perfect embodiment of something.

Oblivious: unaware, clueless, ignorant.

Millicent Bruton

Millicent Bruton, more commonly referred to as Lady Bruton, is an aristocratic woman who often hosts lunch parties. She is 62 years old and lives a life of luxury and prestige. Lady Bruton is a descendent of a military general whose portrait is displayed prominently in her home. This symbolises Lady Bruton's attachment to and respect for traditions. However, Lady Bruton is also restless and desperate to have a greater impact on the world around her.

Lady Bruton's lunch parties are exclusive to wealthy and powerful individuals, typically men. This is because Lady Bruton feels that her life has more purpose and significance when she surrounds herself with important people. She invites Richard Dalloway and Hugh Whitbread to her lunch party but leaves out Clarissa, believing that like many women in society, Clarissa is merely a burden on her husband. Lady Bruton also sees Clarissa's illness as an obstacle to Richard's career progression.

At Lady Bruton's lunch party, Richard and Hugh help her write a letter to the editor of the *Times* to advocate for emigration. Lady Bruton finds meaning in her quest to encourage emigration to Canada. She struggles to express her ideas in words but finds emigration to be an appealing source of liberation and a way of escaping the problems of a changing Great Britain.

Ultimately, Lady Bruton feels that her gender has deprived her of the opportunity to lead in a similar capacity to her ancestor. Her gender has devalued her intelligence and potential as she is excluded from the public realm that she longs for. Lady Bruton understands the limitations of her gender in a repressive society, and as a result, she compromises, choosing to adhere to English traditions whilst seeking to influence the world. This reflects how she is able to conform in a way that allows her to maintain a sense of individuality and her values.

Prime Minister

The Prime Minister of the United Kingdom leads is a figure of traditional institutions. The Prime Minister is never given a name. As a result, he lacks any sort of identity, personality or unique characteristics. He is merely a symbol of English society which has resisted change in the post-war period. He is a **quintessential** representation of the unyielding nature of the British upper class.

Quintessential: a perfect representation of the essence of something.

The Prime Minister is first introduced when his car is moving through the streets of London. It is blocked by an omnibus, unable to progress easily. This reflects the declining power of the aristocratic class, suggesting that its dwindling power is no match for the unstoppable forces of social progress. This undermining of the Prime Minister is furthered when he anticlimactically attends Clarissa's party. None of the guests seem to care about his presence. This disinterest strips the Prime Minister of his significance. Rather than being seen as a powerful leader, he is viewed as a nuisance. There is a sense of desperation as the Prime Minister moves between guests, as if attempting to cling on to power and importance.

The post-war society saw significant scepticism of traditions and substantial social reforms. Society was desperate for change that benefited Britain's citizens, but the ruling class were resistant to these changes. The Prime Minister's portrayal signifies the rapid decline of the British upper class as they were steadfastly opposed to progress. Instead, they remain self-indulgent and more concerned with clinging to their power.

Elizabeth Dalloway

Elizabeth Dalloway is the only child of Clarissa and Richard. She is 17 years old, uncertain about her future, and caught in a struggle between Clarissa and Miss Kilman who both attempt to influence her. Elizabeth is reserved and keeps to herself; she does not want to follow Clarissa's lifestyle, preferring to spend time alone in the country with her father and dogs.

Elizabeth enjoys fantasising about time in the country and a career as possibly a farmer or doctor. She does not enjoy the spotlight like Clarissa and has become religious under Miss Kilman's influence. Miss Kilman teaches Elizabeth about history and exposes her to new ideas and the suffering of the lower class that Elizabeth is **insulated** from. Elizabeth takes an omnibus to the Strand, a street in a working class neighbourhood where Clarissa would never venture. In this journey Elizabeth feels empowered about her future.

Insulated: to be protected from unpleasant experiences.

Elizabeth's sense of duty to Clarissa causes her to abandon the Strand and return home for Clarissa's party. This highlights how Elizabeth is in an uncertain time of forging her identity as she moves towards adult life. There is a sense of hope that Elizabeth has greater opportunities than Clarissa or Miss Kilman due to evolving social values and the expanding role of women. Elizabeth – because she is still young – seems to be the only character who has the potential to thrive in the future. It is not yet known if she too will succumb to the resignation of middle-aged life and the abandonment of her dreams.

Ellie Henderson

Ellie Henderson is Clarissa's cousin and is also in her fifties. Ellie is depicted as being rather ordinary and lacks the prestige and wealth of Clarissa. Clarissa views Ellie's life as bland and uninspiring. Ellie leads a rather **sedentary** lifestyle, unable to move up to a higher social standing, isolated from the extravagance of Clarissa's world. Nevertheless, Ellie is in awe of the affluent lifestyle and asks to attend Clarissa's party.

Sedentary: inactive, mostly motionless.

She is enthralled by the prestigious guests at Clarissa's party, but she mostly remains alone. She is nervous, feels out of place and is unsure of how to engage with others. Richard talks to Ellie for a bit as he felt sympathy for her, but Ellie is seen as aimless as she stays in a corner. She is amazed by the attendance of the Prime Minister and looks forward to telling Edith all about the party. Ellie represents the desire of people to have a sense of belonging and feel important as she absorbs the experience of attending Clarissa's party.

Chapter 5

Key Themes Analysis

Uncertainty and existentialism

The characters in *Mrs Dalloway* are plagued by uncertainty and existential dread. They have experienced the challenges of life and battled the repressive society of the early 20th century. The post-war period embedded a sense of uncertainty as society's rapid changes conflict with longstanding traditions. Woolf interrogates the nature of the human condition and life itself. Woolf's personal struggles with mental health and visions helped her to interrogate human nature and sanity in her writing. The style of *Mrs Dalloway* – through its constant changes in point of view and moving between past and present – extends the overwhelming uncertainty to the reader.

Clarissa faces an identity crisis as she confronts her conventional life in her old age. Her entire sense of self is derived from her role as the perfect hostess. Clarissa aims to impress others, positioning herself as a respectable upper class woman to be admired. Clarissa's doubts about her life choices disturb the stable life she has created. She often looks back at her time at Bourton affectionately wondering what could have been. The sudden return of Peter and Sally illuminates Clarissa's distress and existential dread. She lacks the confidence to pursue her passions uninhibited, so is trapped in an unrelenting state of anxiety.

Peter Walsh returns to London after time in India. Intending to marry Daisy, Peter is conflicted by the resurgence of his feelings for Clarissa that persist deeply within in. His ventures throughout London as he follows a younger woman reflect his nostalgia and yearning for the past. He is desperate to free himself of his attachment to Clarissa but gives in to her invitation to attend her party. This internal conflict showcases the uncertainty Peter faces as his **stagnation** contrasts a rapidly changing world.

Stagnation: not flowing, moving, or developing.

The blissful and passionate relationship of Septimus and Lucrezia was irreparably harmed by the war and its effects on Septimus. The future they had imagined together seems unattainable given the extent of Septimus' illness. Lucrezia fears that she is alone and has lost Septimus forever, whilst Septimus is haunted by the visions and **ravings** of his mind. The uncertainty of Septimus' chances for recovery presents a grim reality that torments Septimus and Lucrezia. This is exacerbated through the dismissiveness of Dr Holmes which denies clarity and rehabilitation.

Ravings: irrational, wild, and incoherent statements.

Miss Kilman's life has been uprooted by the discrimination she faced when standing up for her German heritage. This has led her into misery, resentment and bitterness which manifests in her hatred for Clarissa. Miss Kilman's dissatisfaction with her life makes her insecure and fills her with existential dread. To cope with this, she transforms her sense of inferiority into the belief that she is morally superior to Clarissa. This is furthered through her religious conversion which she uses as a justification of her hatred towards Clarissa. Miss Kilman uses her religion as a shield to mask the bitterness and misery that consumes her. Woolf presents this as a warning to readers to recognise their faults to avoid Miss Kilman's defining existential despair.

The novel ends with great uncertainty as to the futures of each character. In fact, the only character whose ending is certain is Septimus, who takes his own life, unable to endure what he perceives to be the turmoil and cruelty of the world and his own mind. It is possible that characters like Clarissa, Richard and Peter have grown and will more ardently pursue personal fulfilment, but the novel is intentionally **ambiguous** to emphasise that happiness and freedom can only be attained by the active choices of individuals.

Ambiguous: uncertain and unclear, morally grey, or being open to interpretation.

Youthful ambitions

The prominent characters in *Mrs Dalloway* have failed to live up to their youthful dreams. They had ambitions of greatness, freedom, and fierce independence. Yet their aspirations were extinguished as they relented to the ritualistic patterns of life. Their present lives conflict with the profound aspirations that gave their youthful selves passion, hope, and determination. There is a sense of sadness and loss in the way the characters have succumbed to such dreary realities.

Peter had fantasies of becoming a writer and held socialist values at Bourton. This reflects an **idyllic** outlook on life which provides Peter with hope. This vision is undercut by the Peter we see in the present who was never able to fulfil his literary ambitions. Instead, he feels lost, filled with regret and lacking direction.

Idyllic: peaceful, picturesque, and idealistic.

Like Peter, Sally too is far removed from her daring, wild, and adventurous youth. She has ended up marrying a rather ordinary man. Sally's free-spirited nature and desires to transform the world conflicted with the pressures of society. Her abandonment of her fiery self reflects the dichotomy between youthful aspirations and middle-aged resignation. This underscores the important choices people make as their ambitions are challenged and eroded by societal pressures and expectations. Sally has found a middle ground between these powerful forces, and Woolf makes the reader consider the importance of maintaining one's authenticity, pursuing ambitions, and compromising.

In Bourton, Clarissa was ignited by Sally's passion. Sally inspired her to be more outspoken, sincere and daring to reform the world. But like Sally, Clarissa ended up compromising and abandoning her aspirations in favour of a more secure and safe life with Richard. Similarly, Miss Kilman was once enthralled by history but her passion has been undercut by the bitterness that seeped into her life as she experienced social alienation. She is left isolated due to her convictions and has become consumed by religious **fanaticism**, far removed from her youthful ambitions.

Fanaticism: obsessive devotion.

Septimus was caught up in the excitement and allure of the war, believing that it offered a chance to adventure and see the world. Septimus' aspirations were shattered by the war as his mind and spirit were destroyed. He remains a shadow of his former self, deeply tormented by his memories. Septimus feels he can not be healed or loved. With Septimus' hopes and optimism crushed, his ambitions are yet another victim to the harsh reality of the world.

All of the characters are haunted by the past, their failures, the tragic aftermath of World War I, and the inability to fulfil their youthful ambitions. There is an overwhelming sense of misery and despair. The readers are left to grapple with the ambitions and desires of youth with the pressures of society, the demand for conformity and **hegemony**. As the characters have aged and reflect on their lives and circumstances, there is a **romanticisation** or rose-tinted view of the past. The past is glorified as the characters wonder if more ardent pursuits of their youthful dreams could have led to happiness and satisfaction.

Hegemony: the dominance and power of a particular group which influences values, behaviours, and ways of thinking.

Romanticise: to indulge in sentimental nostalgia, making things seem more idealistic.

Suffering and injustice

Mrs Dalloway is littered with suffering and injustice as Woolf depicts a society that is dominated by the wealthy. There is a large power imbalance between the different strata of society. The characters – each facing an existential crisis – are victims of a society that does not value independence and personal fulfilment. The repression of emotions was **endemic** in the aristocracy of British society which pressures people to conform to conventions.

Endemic: widespread or commonly found.

Septimus was destroyed by the horrors of the war, particularly the death of Evans. Upon returning to London, he was unable to return to normal life as he suffered from PTSD and received no support or recognition of his service. Septimus is paralysed by a society that is unable to relate to or understand his experiences. Septimus' internal struggle with his sanity is the result of the derision of doctors and an unrelenting ruling class that seeks to silence him in order to preserve their power and privilege.

Septimus is desperate to communicate his internal suffering to Lucrezia and the world, but finds it impossible to express himself. His decline in sanity is exacerbated by the poor understanding of mental health which saw his condition minimised by Dr Holmes. Septimus and Lucrezia have a deep bond and love for one another, but she can not empathise with him.

This demoralises Lucrezia who feels isolated, unloved, and despondent. Septimus' inability to communicate his suffering with Lucrezia worsens his pain. Woolf emphasises the importance of expression and engaging with one's emotions as essential to dealing with trauma.

Woolf herself had suffered from mental illness. She experienced the dismissive attitude of doctors who merely advised rest and institutionalised her, secluding her from the world. Woolf believed that this isolation from intellectual stimulation is woefully inadequate and not **conducive** to recovery. Septimus reflects the struggle between typical beliefs of masculinity and emotional expression that is necessary to navigate the turmoil and tragedy of war. Septimus' only escape from his suffering is through suicide which emphasises the oppressive nature of society.

Conducive: factors that contribute to making an outcome possible or likely.

Clarissa is restricted by the rigid societal expectations and traditions. Her interpersonal struggles reflect the gender roles that permeated British society at the time. This is furthered through Lady Bruton who feels limited by her gender. Lady Bruton believes she is deprived of power, control, and leadership which causes her substantial grief. Miss Kilman is tormented and ostracised by society. Her obsession with morality and religious purity is a way of covering up her insecurities, and she shields her sense of inferiority with moral righteousness, but the unmistakable suffering leaves her bitter.

Woolf presents a more complex picture of the concept of sanity. She challenges Sir William's notion of proportion and blurs the lines between sanity and insanity. This makes it seem as if no one can truly be sane in a world that seeks to repress and control people. Clarissa is paralleled to Septimus as they both struggle with mental illness and suicidal thoughts. Despite never meeting, they are united in their consistent battle for control and contentment. Septimus and Clarissa's shared struggles suggest that suffering, isolation, and insanity is an inescapable reality for all in a world that does not value authenticity.

Appearance and reputation

Humans tend to give great attention to their appearance and the image they present. Difficulties arise when this image conflicts with one's identity or requires compromising one's individuality. Given the strict societal expectations in the 1920s of following traditions and maintaining a pure reputation, many characters in *Mrs Dalloway* appear obsessed with their appearance. Woolf seeks to expose this as a fruitless pursuit that may make one feel more secure and well-adjusted to society but fails to yield satisfaction.

Clarissa is fearful of being isolated from the social circles she is desperate to be a part of. She has spent her life crafting a façade of nobility and strength. Clarissa is desperate to be admired and fears social invisibility. This is evident through Clarissa's anxiety about not receiving an invitation to Lady Bruton's lunch party. Clarissa seeks to evade her insecurity and mortality by hosting parties and mingling with aristocrats. However, beyond the exterior Clarissa presents, she is plagued by uncertainty and insecurity.

Peter and Sally are more willing to express their personality and emotions than Clarissa. They think more critically of the world around them and, as a result, are particularly critical of Clarissa. Peter's disapproving stare affects Clarissa and reminds her of her insincerity. Sally speaks boldly against the shortcomings of society. Together, Peter and Sally are distinguished from the other characters who insist on working within society's stringent framework.

Like Clarissa, Hugh's personality revolves around his reputation. He has a job at court which mostly consists of running errands, yet he takes great pride in the feeling that his job is valuable and significant. Sir William has a **stellar** reputation for his methodical approach to his patients. He takes joy in the power he exerts over others similarly to Dr Holmes. Dr Holmes is indifferent to Septimus' suffering, and after Septimus' suicide, he chose to preserve his reputation as a respected practitioner. Dr Holmes drugs Lucrezia and distances himself from responsibility for Septimus' death when talking with Mrs Filmer.

Stellar: outstanding and high in quality.

There is often a great divide between a person's appearance and the reality within. Woolf explores this by engaging with the interpersonal struggles of each character. Readers get an insight into the lives and internal monologues of characters like Clarissa, Peter and Septimus. It becomes clear that these characters are fractured and grappling with problems that threaten their reputation and sense of self. Ultimately, Woolf encourages readers to focus more on themselves than obsessing over attaining a **palatable** image.

Palatable: agreeable, acceptable, or tasteful.

Love and human connection

The novel emphasises how human connection is vital to one's happiness and purpose in life. It is what binds people together and enables empathy, joy, and hope. Without love and connection to others, people tend to feel secluded, unworthy, and dejected. Peter's life seems to be defined by his longing for Clarissa and the ever-present pain within him from her rejection. Septimus and Lucrezia are deeply in love, but their relationship is crushed by the weight of Septimus' abandonment by society. Woolf represents expressing love for others as a form of genuine communication that is key to fulfillment.

At Bourton, Clarissa experienced authentic and passionate love for Sally. Sally exposed Clarissa to new, radical ideas which challenged orthodox ways of thinking. This instilled in Clarissa a desire to live a freer life defined by herself rather than society. The impact Sally had highlights how love and companionship can shape one's beliefs, aspirations, and sense of self. The clash between Sally's bold **reformist** vision and conventions caused Clarissa to choose to marry Richard, the traditional and ordinary man, instead of Peter, who is the more emotionally sensitive of the two. Clarissa's choice of Richard contributes to her sense of uncertainty and thoughts of what could have been different had she pursued unbridled, passionate love rather than what was practical.

Reformist: someone who supports or advocates for change.

Woolf also interrogates the concept of privacy within a relationship. The idea of a gulf existing between a husband and wife appears to undermine the unity of marriage, but the reality Woolf presents is more ambiguous. The gulf between Septimus and Lucrezia – which has formed due to Septimus' mental illness – is destructive as it alienates them and inhibits communication. Their relationship is strained, leaving them both feeling unworthy, unloved and not valued. By contrast, the gulf between Clarissa and Richard is presented as healthy and a necessary balance. They have their separate lives but remain committed to each other, although Richard does struggle directly tell Clarissa that he loves her.

Woolf explores the need for companionship by representing the devastating impacts of isolation. Peter is isolated as he can not get over Clarissa's rejection. Septimus and Lucrezia feel isolated as their worldviews conflict as Septimus' condition deteriorates. This accentuates the importance of communication as a means of alleviating suffering and enhancing connection. Septimus is unable to express to Lucrezia the intense pain he experiences. This is catastrophic as Septimus feels his only true act of communication is through suicide.

Power and control

People tend to desire having power and influence; there is a sense of achievement and satisfaction when one has control over their life. The human desires for control and self-determination are explored in *Mrs Dalloway* where these desires are threatened by a repressive society. The society is structured so that those with wealth have immense power and conformity is viewed as necessary. This hinders individuality and often leads to characters like Clarissa and Lady Bruton feeling trapped by the expectations thrust upon them.

Clarissa enjoys being adored by others and having control of her life. Her relationship with Elizabeth, however, is threatened by Miss Kilman's influence. Clarissa perceives Miss Kilman to be an oppressive force who challenges Clarissa's power over Elizabeth. Elizabeth is rather **impressionable** which puts her at odds with both Clarissa and Miss Kilman. Elizabeth tries to remain neutral in their conflicts and desires freedom and escape. She fantasises of time in the country. There is hope that Elizabeth will have a greater capacity than Clarissa to determine her fate, especially due to the changing roles of women in society.

Impressionable: easily influenced by others.

Septimus has lost control as he has descended into insanity. Lucrezia places her trust in doctors and institutions to help Septimus, but they are ultimately let down. Septimus' suicide is his way of taking control of his life and escaping the oppressive forces of Dr Holmes and Sir William. It is a form of freedom that Clarissa has actively sacrificed to preserve her image and reputation.

People like Hugh and Sir William embrace traditional forms of power and take pride in this. They represent the tendency of elites to cling to power and traditions. The consequence of maintaining this power is that is suppresses the lower class and keeps them vulnerable and powerless. Hugh and Sir William are presented as egotistical and apathetic to the suffering of others. Peter and Sally appear to be more free-spirited, but they are alienated from society as they tend to break conventions. Woolf explores this dichotomy between freedom and exclusion.

The characters face difficulty in having **dominion** over their lives. They yearn for autonomy, but their identities are held hostage to societal pressures. Their nature, exterior, and beliefs are moulded by society and pressures to conform. This conflict between individualism and conformity is at the heart of the novel. Woolf explores the detriments of having a lack of control, thus encouraging readers to seek control of their lives.

Dominion: to have control or power over something.

The novel presents a bleak view of the world. Woolf presents a core conflict where people must choose between expressions of individuality and conforming. Individuality is viewed as risky and leading to isolation, whereas conformity oppresses independence and emotional sensitivity. Ultimately, Woolf encourages readers to sustain a private life which provides the opportunity to be in touch with one's emotions and imagination. Woolf views this as critical to finding peace within oneself and staying sane in a controlled society.

The passing of time

Whilst *Mrs Dalloway* explores a single day, flashbacks capture the changes that have occurred as many years have passed. Many of the characters are facing the realities of their old age, having to grapple with missed opportunities, regret and a sense of purposelessness. Confronted with the inevitability of death, one has the opportunity for **introspection** to re-evaluate one's life and future.

Introspection: self-reflection of one's thoughts and feelings.

The passing of time amplifies the struggles of characters as they become increasingly sombre, unfulfilled and mournful. The motif of clocks serve as a constant reminder of time and pressures characters to reflect as they confront their mortality. The striking of clocks are often used to shift the perspective from one character to another. As this happens, the reader comes to realise that Clarissa, Peter, Septimus, Lady Bruton, Miss Kilman, and others are all fearful that their decisions have left them irrevocably trapped.

Woolf also explores how one's identity evolves with time and is shaped by the past. Flashbacks are used extensively to show how one's identity is feud with their past selves. Clarissa is constantly thinking about what could have been. She is deeply attached to her past life in Bourton which represents liberation and agency. Peter is unable to move on from Clarissa and is haunted by her rejection, while Septimus' life has been upturned by his horrific experiences in the war and he is left dejected, deeply distressed, and suffering from PTSD.

The passing of time also highlights the changes to society. The immense social upheaval caused by the war meant change was necessary to deal with the turmoil. The expansion of the middle class, an increase in women's rights, and the spread of democracy saw a decline in the power of the British Empire. This creates tension as the ruling class attempts to preserve its authority and relevance. The modernisation of society is noted by Peter who is in awe of summer time and the respect people have for ambulances.

The emphasis on time pressures the characters and readers to make changes to their lives. They are pressured to either change or remain transfixed by self-pity, insecurity, and uncertainty. There is some hope created at the novel's conclusion that – despite old age – there still remains an opportunity to seek genuine fulfilment. Clarissa is **galvanised** to find satisfaction and meaning, Richard is more expressive of his love, Sally is in touch with her emotions, and Peter has a sense of enthusiasm for the future. They simply need to have the will to fight against temptations to conform to find personal fulfilment. In this way, one can transcend the boundaries and rigidity of time.

Galvanised: to be spurred into suddenly acting.

Chapter 6

Structural Features Analysis

The events of *Mrs Dalloway* take place over a single, rather ordinary day. Rather than a fast-paced plot or traditional narrative structure, it is the characters and their reflections on the world and their lives that drive the story. Woolf intentionally chose to focus predominately on the inner minds of each character rather than their carefully crafted exteriors. Woolf uses flashbacks and shifting perspectives to produce fractured images that highlight the complexities of society and each character. These images are ambiguous, and the reader is left to decipher and evaluate them.

The uncertainty that Woolf creates is amplified by the novel's style. The characters are unreliable narrators and each have their own biases. The novel often makes it difficult to discern whose perspective it is. Lengthy sentences that appear unending create vivid descriptions and contribute to the personal feel of a character's internal monologue. Woolf's writing is emotive and challenging as characters **oscillate** between the past and present. This contributes to rich imagery, meaning, and reflection within the novel.

Oscillate: to sway back and forth between two things.

Form and Modernism

In Woolf's era, men established and inhabited all literary spaces, creating a community of prestige which made it difficult for women to enter. As a writer, Woolf went against these conventional literary structures and beliefs about how stories should be told. Woolf presented female characters with greater complexity, depth, and individuality. This is particularly evident through Clarissa whose motivations are intricately examined and scrutinised.

The style Woolf uses enables a more comprehensive and compassionate portrayal of human consciousness. Woolf deviates from conventional structures in order to interrogate human desires and suffering in a more authentic way for readers. She delves inside the inner worlds of each character to show their past and current identities. It is through this fusion of past and present that Woolf gives voice and agency to her characters despite the plot taking place over just one day.

Woolf challenged literary traditions by experimenting in narrative form. In the 1800s, literary conventions were much more rigid in terms of structure and style. Woolf was passionate in telling a story that provoked critical reflection in readers. A neatly systematic story, Woolf believed, was inadequate in reflecting the shattered reality of the contemporary psyche. Woolf utilised a non-linear structure to capture the **entrenched** disarray of the time in a more realistic way.

Entrenched: deeply embedded and firmly established.

Mrs Dalloway is also a classic Modernist novel – Modernism refers to the literary and philosophical movement of the late 1800s and early 1900s that responded to rapid industrialisation, increasing urbanisation, and developing technology. Modernism reflects the upheaval of World War I and the significant forces within society propelling change and progress. Like Woolf, Modernist writers sought to make sense of the world. At its core, Modernism was about the search for meaning in an unstable, uncertain world. This often resulted in critiques of prevailing traditions, encouraging scepticism, and exploring disillusionment. Woolf depicted the traditional structures and institutions of society as inherently repressive, unequal, and immoral.

Because Modernist writers challenged the systems of society, they innovated with new narrative structures. This deviation from traditional writing helped to distinguish modernist texts from more classical literature. In Woolf's writing, the focus is almost entirely on characters, their experiences, and their perspectives on the world. The novel transcends plot and delves more deeply into the psyche of each character. Woolf experimented with style and form to create a genuine, authentic novel that emulated her experiences. Woolf felt let down by institutions as she suffered with her mental health but was dismissed and failed by doctors. This apathy inspires Woolf's writing, particularly Dr Holmes and Sir William's cruelty.

Flashbacks

The most mundane activities or moments can stimulate a flashback or memory. For example, when Clarissa walks along Bond street at the beginning of the novel, she remembers her father buying a suit from a shop on the street. This fills her with joy and reflects how she longs for the happiness of her past.

Flashbacks are used frequently to create **nuance** to an otherwise basic, chronological storyline. Current events are often disrupted by flashbacks or sudden memories which deepen the reader's understanding of how characters are shaped by their pasts. This engages the reader, developing curiosity and intrigue as they are drawn into the lives of each character. Woolf desires readers to sympathise with the pain and perspective of her characters to present a less straightforward view of the world. This is particularly true with Septimus where flashbacks of a more joyful, optimistic, and lively figure are undercut by his present scarred self.

Nuance: subtle details or complexities.

The flashbacks Woolf uses establish background information about characters and events that affect the present day. This allows for a more intimate connection between the characters and the reader, and convey their nostalgia for bygone days, exacerbated by their current dissatisfaction. This is mostly done through flashbacks to youth which reveals the extensive impact the past has on one's identity.

Clarissa is a very private individual and hides her true thoughts and feelings from others. Flashbacks create a window for the reader to peer into the inner life of Clarissa as opposed to more conventional methods of **explicitly** telling the reader her thoughts and motivations.

Explicitly: in a direct and exact way, with no ambiguity.

The bulk of the flashbacks are from Bourton where we see Clarissa's relationships with Sally, Peter, and Richard develop. This creates a large gap in the story between current events and the events at Bourton. There is no information given of what happens in between; Clarissa's marriage to Richard, the birth of Elizabeth, and Richard's entrance into politics are left untold. The enormous void between the present and Bourton – during which time Clarissa's identity has been altered dramatically – accentuates the immense transition Clarissa has undergone. It is left for the reader to speculate, but is this shift is likely to exemplify the necessity of women adapting to a patriarchal culture that is repressive.

It is also through flashbacks to Bourton that readers come to understand Clarissa's aspirations and desires. Although she marries Richard, he does not feature prominently in Clarissa's flashbacks and fond memories; instead, the focus is on Sally and Peter. Clarissa reminisces on her passionate love for Sally whose adventurous spirit inspired and invigorated her. She also laments rejecting Peter's proposal for marriage. This rejection has stuck with Peter and is a constant source of insecurity and pain. It is through Peter's flashbacks that the reader sees Richard's pursuit of Clarissa and the demise of Peter and Clarissa's relationship. Readers must sort through flashbacks and different perspectives to appreciate the complexity of Woolf's characters.

Point of view

Mrs Dalloway is written in the point of view of a third person **omniscient** narrator. This means that the narrator is not a character in the story, but a separate entity that has access to all information and perspectives. Woolf also repeatedly switches between an omniscient narrator and the point of view of multiple characters. This gives Woolf the freedom to tell the story in an intimate and controlled way. These shifts in perspective are seamless, so it can be difficult for readers to know exactly whose point of view they are getting.

Omniscient: having unlimited knowledge and complete awareness.

The point of view often changes **erratically**, typically moving at a single point in time between characters. For example, when a crowd had gathered outside Buckingham Palace as a plane wrote letters in the sky, the perspective moves quickly from one character to the next. Woolf uses events like this that attract the attention of many people to show different perspectives. This style highlights the interconnectedness of people and **foregrounds** the commonality of humanity and suffering. It emphasises how people are all bound by the same problems and fears despite having vastly different experiences and backgrounds.

Erratically: irregular, uncontrolled, or unpredictable.

Foregrounds: to make something appear more prominent.

Each character has their own biases and version of events. This makes them **unreliable narrators**. This is especially true for Septimus whose mental illness causes delirious visions, making it difficult for him to distinguish between delusions and reality. Since the entire novel is told from a range of points of view, readers only receive limited information. Woolf's intention is not to provide a factual account, but rather engage the reader deeply with the lives of each character to understand their place in the world.

Unreliable narration: a literary technique where characters have a limited and potentially untrustworthy point of view.

Stream of consciousness

One of the major innovations of Modernist literature was the stream of consciousness style. This is where the writer attempts to capture the thoughts and emotions of a character as though they were a continuous flow, often not adhering to typical rules of **syntax** and punctuation. This is typically done as an internal monologue with lengthy, drawn-out sentences to mirror the way people's thoughts drift from one thing to another. In Woolf's writing, there is no uniform structure, but constant shifts between the past and present to reflect the emotions and thoughts of each character. Woolf sought to authentically imitate the human mind and personal anguish through her stream of consciousness style.

Syntax: the rules of grammar and sentence structure.

When a character's stream of consciousness involves reflecting on an event, it can be difficult to discern between the past and present. This is because of how **organically** Woolf depicts thoughts as effortlessly moving between ideas and time periods. This is done deliberately to merge the past and present, demonstrating they are inseparable from one's identity. Thus, this stream of consciousness technique provides a glimpse into the way characters feel, think, and justify their actions.

Organically: happening in a natural way, without being forced.

Chapter 7

Quote Bank

Key Point :
Remember that these section numbers are not part of the text itself so are only included to help you locate the quotes if needed. If you need to search the novel for a particular quote or moment, I would recommend using a digital version such as the one provided by Project Gutenberg (https://gutenberg.net.au/ebooks02/0200991h.html).

Uncertainty and existentialism

Quote	Section
"Did it matter then, [Clarissa] asked herself, walking towards Bond Street, did it matter that she must inevitably cease completely; all this must go on without her; did she resent it; or did it not become consoling to believe that death ended absolutely?"	1
"And Maisie Johnson, as she joined that gently trudging, vaguely gazing, breeze-kissed company—squirrels perching and preening, sparrow fountains fluttering for crumbs, dogs busy with the railings, busy with each other, while the soft warm air washed over them and lent to the fixed unsurprised gaze with which they received life something whimsical and mollified"	2
"Her voice, being the voice of the hostess, is reluctant to inflict its individuality. Some grief for the past holds it back; some concern for the present."	4
"What is it? Where am I? And why, after all, does one do it? [Peter] thought, the divorce seeming all moonshine."	4
"He liked continuity; and the sense of handing on the traditions of the past. It was a great age in which to have lived."	8
"And in the large square where the cabs shot and swerved so quick, there were loitering couples, dallying, embracing, shrunk up under the shower of a tree; that was moving; so silent, so absorbed, that one passed, discreetly, timidly, as if in the presence of some sacred ceremony to interrupt which would have been impious."	11

"[Ellie] herself having always been a wisp of a creature, with her thin hair and meagre profile; though now, past fifty, there was beginning to shine through some mild beam, something purified into distinction by years of self-abnegation but obscured again, perpetually, by her distressing gentility, her panic fear."	12
"Then (she had felt it only this morning) there was the terror; the overwhelming incapacity, one's parents giving it into one's hands, this life, to be lived to the end, to be walked with serenely; there was in the depths of her heart an awful fear."	12

Youthful ambitions

Quote	Section
"Perhaps at midnight, when all boundaries are lost, the country reverts to its ancient shape, as the Romans saw it, lying cloudy, when they landed, and the hills had no names and rivers wound they knew not where—such was [Lucrezia's] darkness."	2
"[Peter] had been a Socialist, in some sense a failure—true. Still the future of civilisation lies, he thought, in the hands of young men like that; of young men such as he was, thirty years ago; with their love of abstract principles."	4
"Down, down [Peter] sank into the plumes and feathers of sleep, sank, and was muffled over."	4
"The feet of those people busy about their activities, hands putting stone to stone, minds eternally occupied not with trivial chatterings...but with thoughts of ships, of business, of law, of administration."	9
"As a child suddenly stretches its arms; it was just that, perhaps, a sigh, a stretch of the arms, an impulse, a revelation, which has its effects for ever, and then down again it went to the sandy floor. [Elizabeth] must go home."	9
"But [Sally's] voice was wrung of its old ravishing richness; her eyes not aglow as they used to be."	12

Suffering and injustice

Quote	Section
"[Clarissa] had a perpetual sense, as she watched the taxi cabs, of being out, out, far out to sea and alone."	1
"The sheet was stretched and the bed narrow. [Clarissa] had gone up into the tower alone and left them blackberrying in the sun."	3
"[Lucrezia] was like a bird sheltering under the thin hollow of a leaf, who blinks at the sun when the leaf moves; starts at the crack of a dry twig."	6
"[Septimus'] body was macerated until only the nerve fibres were left. It was spread like a veil upon a rock."	6
"The War had taught [Septimus]. It was sublime. He had gone through the whole show, friendship, European War, death, had won promotion, was still under thirty and was bound to survive. He was right there. The last shells missed him. He watched them explode with indifference."	6
"[Human beings] hunt in packs. Their packs scour the desert and vanish screaming into the wilderness. They desert the fallen. They are plastered over with grimaces."	6
"She should have been in a factory; behind a counter; Mrs. Dalloway and all the other fine ladies!"	9
"There remained only the window... the tiresome, the troublesome, and rather melodramatic business of opening the window and throwing himself out."	10
"These triumphs... had a hollowness; at arm's length they were, not in the heart; and it might be that [Clarissa] was growing old but they satisfied her no longer as they used."	12
"if ever a woman could have worn the helmet and shot the arrow, could have led troops to attack, ruled with indomitable justice barbarian hordes and lain under a shield noseless in a church, or made a green grass mound on some primeval hillside, that woman was Millicent Bruton. Debarred by her sex, and some truancy, too, of the logical faculty."	12
"It was [Clarissa's] punishment to see sink and disappear here a man, there a woman, in this profound darkness, and she forced to stand here in her evening dress."	12

Appearance and reputation

Quote	Section
"The Queen herself held up; the Queen herself unable to pass."	2
"Let rumour accumulate in their veins and thrill the nerves in their thighs at the thought of Royalty looking at them; the Queen bowing; the Prince saluting."	2
"But they beckoned; leaves were alive; trees were alive. And the leaves being connected by millions of fibres with Septimus' own body."	2
"Away and away the aeroplane shot, till it was nothing but a bright spark; an aspiration; a concentration; a symbol."	2
"It was Clarissa one remembered. Not that she was striking; not beautiful at all; there was nothing picturesque about her; she never said anything specially clever; there she was, however; there she was."	6
"[Clarissa] frittered her time away, lunching, dining, giving these incessant parties of hers, talking nonsense, sayings things she didn't mean, blunting the edge of her mind, losing her discrimination."	6
"[Peter] had come back, battered, unsuccessful, to their secure shores. But to help him, they reflected, was impossible; there was some flaw in his character."	8
"Did it matter, did it matter in the least, one Prime Minister more or less?"	12
"One couldn't laugh at [the Prime Minister]. He looked so ordinary."	12
"But age had brushed [Clarissa]; even as a mermaid might behold in her glass the setting sun on some very clear evening over the waves."	12

Love and human connection

Quote	Section
"There was nobody. [Lucrezia's] words faded. So a rocket fades. Its sparks, having grazed their way into the night, surrender to it, dark descends, pours over the outlines of houses and towers; bleak hillsides soften and fall in."	2
"If it were now to die 'twere now to be most happy."	3

"[Peter] felt that he was grinding against something physically hard; [Clarissa] was unyielding. She was like iron, like flint, rigid up the backbone."	5
"Unable to get away from the thought of [Clarissa]; she kept coming back and back like a sleeper jolting against [Peter] in a railway carriage."	6
"[Lucrezia] was a flowering tree; and through her branches looked out the face of a lawgiver, who had reached a sanctuary where she feared no one."	10
"[Clarissa] had felt that intoxication of the moment, that dilatation of the nerves of the heart itself till it seemed to quiver."	12
"What is it that fills me with extraordinary excitement? It is Clarissa, he said. For there she was."	12

Power and control

Quote	Section
"The world has raised its whip; where will it descend?"	2
"The world wavered and quivered and threatened to burst into flames."	2
"Such are the visions which proffer great cornucopias full of fruit to the solitary traveller, or murmur in his ear like sirens lolloping away on the green sea waves, or are dashed in his face like bunches of roses, or rise to the surface like pale faces which fishermen flounder through floods to embrace."	5
"The passing generations—the pavement was crowded with bustling middle-class people—vanished, like leaves, to be trodden under, to be soaked and steeped and made mould of by that eternal spring."	6
"Worshipping proportion, Sir William not only prospered himself but made England prosper, secluded her lunatics, forbade childbirth, penalised despair, made it impossible for the unfit to propagate their views until they, too, shared his sense of proportion."	7
"But Proportion has a sister, less smiling, more formidable, a Goddess...Conversion is her name and she feasts on the wills of the weakly, loving to impress, to impose, adoring her own features stamped on the face of the populace."	7
"Richard turned at the corner of Conduit Street eager, yes, very eager, to travel that spider's thread of attachment between himself and Clarissa."	8

"And now it was like riding, to be rushing up Whitehall; and to each movement of the omnibus the beautiful body in the fawn-coloured coat responded freely like a rider... and [Elizabeth's] fine eyes, having no eyes to meet, gazed ahead, blank, bright, with the staring incredible innocence of sculpture."	9
"[The Prime Minister] tried to look somebody. It was amusing to watch. Nobody looked at him. They just went on talking, yet it was perfectly plain that they all knew, felt to the marrow of their bones, this majesty passing; this symbol of what they all stood for, English society."	12
"Death was defiance. Death was an attempt to communicate; people feeling the impossibility of reaching the centre which, mystically, evaded them; closeness drew apart; rapture faded, one was alone. There was an embrace in death."	12

The passing of time

Quote	Section
"[Clarissa] felt very young; at the same time unspeakably aged. She sliced like a knife through everything; at the same time was outside, looking on."	1
"As they looked the whole world became perfectly silent, and a flight of gulls crossed the sky, first one gull leading, then another, and in this extraordinary silence and peace, in this pallor, in this purity, bells struck eleven times, the sound fading up there among the gulls."	2
"But [Clarissa] feared time itself, and read on Lady Bruton's face, as if it had been a dial cut in impassive stone, the dwindling of life; how year by year her share was sliced."	3
"The word "time" split its husk; poured its riches over [Septimus]; and from his lips fell like shells, like shavings from a plane."	6
"It was precisely twelve o'clock; twelve by Big Ben; whose stroke was wafted over the northern part of London; blent with that of other clocks, mixed in a thin ethereal way with the clouds and wisps of smoke, and died up there among the seagulls."	7
"The sound of Big Ben flooded Clarissa's drawing-room."	8
"Volubly, troublously, the late clock sounded."	9

Chapter 8

Sample Essays

Essay One

QUESTION: Analyse how Virginia Woolf's *Mrs Dalloway* explores the nature of suffering.

ESSAY	COMMENTS
INTRODUCTION Virginia Woolf's *Mrs Dalloway* presents suffering as an inevitability in a repressive society.[1] Set in the 1920s, *Mrs Dalloway* explores a world where the aristocrats are desperate to hold onto their power. They seek to preserve traditional institutions at the expense of the lower class whose individuality is suppressed. The novel explores how suffering is endemic and caused by societal pressures to conform, poor mental health, and due to lacking identity and security.[2] Therefore, Woolf portrays suffering as an inevitable challenge that requires strength and support to overcome.[3]	1. The first sentence immediately addresses the essay question, and expresses a clear interpretation or thesis statement, rather than simply restating the question. This is essential for a strong introduction. 2. These three main points are introduced as clear supporting arguments for our thesis. They are succinct, without any unnecessary detail (save the analysis for your body paragraphs where you can earn marks for it!). 3. This sentence links back to the thesis and the question, focusing on Woolf's overarching intent.

PARAGRAPH 1

Society places pressure on individuals to conform, whilst people who resist are often secluded and scorned. This forces people to choose between maintaining or compromising their individuality.[4] Woolf explores this challenge and the widespread suffering this causes. Clarissa Dalloway has actively chosen to abandon her youthful ambitions for a more secure, safe life. This self-imposed isolation is evident through Clarissa's reflections, "as she watched the taxi cabs, of being out, out, far out to sea and alone". The movement of taxi cabs symbolise progression and evolution that conflicts with Clarissa's immobility.[5] Like Clarissa, Peter is also stationary in life and suffering from a lack of direction.[6] Peter returned "battered, unsuccessful, to their secure shores" which highlights the tragedy of his state. He has suffered through seclusion as he has staunchly refused to conform to society's standards. Millicent Bruton and Hugh Whitbread see Peter's emotional sensitivity as a weakness, "some flaw in his character" as they value stability and status over individuality.[7] Sally Seton is similarly well-connected to her emotions like Peter. She has sacrificed her wild, daring youth which has dulled her essence as "her voice was wrung of its old ravishing richness; her eyes not aglow as they used to be". This metaphorically presents Sally's transition into a conventionally respectable woman as not worthwhile as her individuality has suffered.[8] Through Clarissa, Peter and Sally, Woolf depicts the suffering caused by the clash of individuality and conformity.

4. A broad overview of the point is given before moving into the text. This helps with structure and developing a conceptual response.
5. The analysis uses evidence from the text and a technique. Most importantly, the technique's effect is explained.
6. When moving to a new piece of evidence, use linking words and ensure that there is a clear connection between the points.
7. Peter's return is explained in terms of his suffering which directly responds to the question.
8. A wide range of characters have been analysed to show the widespread suffering. This is important in developing the thesis which argues that suffering is inevitable.

PARAGRAPH 2	
Struggles with mental health harms an individual's sense of self, happiness and their relationships. In *Mrs Dalloway*, mental illness is viewed as a personal failure which exacerbates personal suffering. Septimus Warren Smith has served his country honourably in war, but the horrors he experienced have left him damaged and fearful.[9] Septimus has been abandoned by society, leaving him vulnerable to mental illness and insanity through post-traumatic stress disorder (PTSD). The rhetorical question in "the world has raised its whip; where will it descend?" highlights Septimus' powerlessness to the oppressive force of society. He is isolated, left to suffer intensely with no hope of rehabilitation or escape. This destroys his blissful relationship with Lucrezia as they are unable to communicate and enjoy peaceful life.[10] Lucrezia is left helpless to the destructive power of Septimus' declining mental state as "She was like a bird sheltering under the thin hollow of a leaf". This simile represents her vulnerability to suffering from a cruel, unforgiving world that has devastated Septimus. Septimus does not receive proper treatment from medical institutions which erodes hope for Septimus and Lucrezia.[11] Septimus' visions have distorted Septimus' worldview and sense of reality. They cause his body to be "spread like a veil upon a rock." This simile represents how Septimus has been victimised by a society that has abandoned him. He is unable to communicate with the world and is suffering immense trauma. The total demolition of Septimus' identity and personality reflects the suffering that civilisation reinforces on individuals struggling with mental health.[12]	9. Some brief contextual information is given about Septimus before the analysis. You are allowed to assume that your marker is familiar with the text (so you don't need to explain his entire backstory) but it is often useful to show the assessor that you understand which details are relevant for your discussion. 10. Septimus' suffering is discussed in two ways: powerlessness and a damaged relationship. This is an ideal scope for a body paragraph as it's not too narrow and not too broad. 11. This analysis of Lucrezia shows that the pain she experiences as a result of their damaged relationship and Septimus' mental illness. 12. The paragraph ends with clear linking of the point back to the thesis and the question.

PARAGRAPH 3	
A repressive society enforces expectations on individuals to maintain a status of nobility and class. This causes insecurity and threatens one's identity. Still tormented by Clarissa's rejection, Peter is unsure of his purpose and place in the world. After chasing a younger woman in the streets of London, he became tired and "down, down he sank into the plumes and feathers of sleep." The imagery conveys a swift loss of energy and lethargy portrays Peter's loss of identity. He lacks the vitality of life as he is consumed by nostalgia, still deeply affected by Clarissa.[13] Like Peter, Doris Kilman is an outsider who has suffered from society's harsh seclusion. Miss Kilman lost her job because she defended her German heritage. This led Miss Kilman to a deeply dissatisfied life where she lives vicariously through Elizabeth Dalloway. Miss Kilman despises Clarissa and copes with her suffering through religious fanaticism and the belief that she is morally superior to Clarissa. Clarissa unnerves Miss Kilman as, in her presence, Miss Kilman "lost her malignity, her size." She is filled with a sense of inadequacy, making her envious of Clarissa's affluence and comfortable lifestyle. Miss Kilman uses her perceived religious purity as a way of suppressing her inferiority. Elizabeth is torn between the influence of Clarissa and Miss Kilman. After contemplating her ambitions and future, Elizabeth returns home to attend Clarissa's party. Her resignation to mediocrity and expectations is symbolised by the omnibuses which "suddenly lost their glow." Elizabeth's ambitions to pursue a life on her own terms remains a tantalising dream. Woolf presents the complexity of suffering through these characters to suggest that insecurity can be self-imposed.[14]	13. Peter's suffering is manifested in physical exhaustion. This emphasises his age and distance from the past he yearns for. 14. Miss Kilman's personal suffering due to her insecurity is more complex because she uses her religious righteousness to mask her suffering. This leads to Elizabeth feeling trapped between the forces of Clarissa and Miss Kilman, thereby conveying how suffering can be perpetuated across characters and generations.

CONCLUSION In a repressive society where individuality is suppressed, suffering is an inevitable reality. Suffering can be personal through challenges with mental health, insecurity and identity. Suffering can also be through societal pressures to conform and exclusion for not adhering to expectations. The characters of Clarissa, Peter, and Sally have changed drastically since their youth, but they are united in their struggles to find purpose and fulfilment. The different lives each character leads and their pain reflects the inevitability of suffering.[15]	15. The conclusion reinforces the thesis, sums up the main points and directly explains the nature of suffering in *Mrs Dalloway.*

Essay Two

QUESTION: Clarissa Dalloway's life is described by Peter Walsh as a pursuit to become the perfect hostess. To what extent do you agree with his statement?

ESSAY	COMMENTS
INTRODUCTION In Virginia Woolf's *Mrs Dalloway*, Clarissa Dalloway is obsessed with her status and reputation. She desires admiration and respect, manifesting in her role as the perfect hostess. However, to achieve this, Clarissa sacrifices her individuality for conformity. This enables Clarissa to fit in with the upper class and become entrenched in elitist social circles. Clarissa's parties provide Clarissa with comfort and validation, represent her insecurity and fears, and reflect her innate ambitions to be venerated.[1] Whilst Clarissa has actively pursued the role of the perfect hostess, this pursuit is simply a way of achieving influence and admiration.[2]	1. This question requires us to focus almost entirely on Clarissa. Therefore the argument must make a judgement as to Clarissa's nature in terms of wanting to become the perfect hostess. 2. The final sentence of the introduction introduces a counterargument. It argues that Clarissa is solely motivated by admiration and having influence, not becoming the perfect hostess. Her role as a hostess, then, is just a convenient form of attaining this adoration.

PARAGRAPH 1

Clarissa uses her parties as a way of escaping her inner fears of loneliness and attaining validation. Clarissa surrounds herself with people to make herself feel special, important and valued.[3] Clarissa's party is an opportunity for her to honour herself. She is desperate to present a façade of strength so people don't see "the other sides of her—faults, jealousies, vanities, suspicions." Clarissa is obsessed with presenting a pure image of confidence, however, Clarissa's discontent is well entrenched and can not be quelled by parties.[4] Clarissa's younger self had bold aspirations of transforming the world, inspired by Sally Seton's authentic and daring nature. Clarissa's pursuit of being the perfect hostess saw her abandon her ambitions for an exciting and fulfilling life as she "frittered her time away... losing her discrimination." The metaphor highlights how Clarissa's need to please others and form an image of respectability supersedes her individuality. Woolf uses Clarissa's parties to represent her prioritisation of her public exterior as the perfect hostess. This exposes Clarissa's exterior as a way of distracting herself from insecurity and dissatisfaction. The Prime Minister's attendance at the party invigorates Clarissa as "she had felt that intoxication of the moment, that dilatation of the nerves of the heart." This metaphor focuses the reader's attention on Clarissa's pride as she flaunts the prestige of her party.[5] To the reader, Clarissa's fragility is transparent as she masks her insecurity with adoration as part of the upper class. This represents Clarissa's desperate attempts to feel validated and self-assured as the perfect hostess.[6]

3. Very specific language is used to describe Clarissa. This conveys our interpretation of the text as well as our deep understanding of the character.
4. This part focuses on Clarissa's façade which she has created to hide her flaws.
5. The contrast between Clarissa's youthful aspirations and present self represents the power of her desire for status.
6. This part connects the analysis to the reader's point of view, reflecting the purpose of Woolf's construction of Clarissa.

PARAGRAPH 2 Clarissa's pursuit of status and recognition has exacerbated her insecurity as she is vulnerable to the judgement of others. She has lost part of her identity which torments her. Clarissa's life is rigidly controlled. She is fearful of being authentic due to pressures to conform. Her devotion to the role of the perfect hostess renders her voice being "reluctant to inflict its individuality." The personification of Clarissa's voice emphasises her lack of confidence and how she has restricted her personality to best fit her façade.[7] Peter Walsh is critical of Clarissa's façade which causes Clarissa discomfort when he stares at her. Peter serves as a symbol of Clarissa's past and how she can not separate her instincts from her identity. Clarissa's fear of losing her status makes her emotionally distant and unwilling to sincerely express herself. This is clear when Peter confessed his love for Clarissa: she "was unyielding. She was like iron, like flint, rigid up the backbone." The similes symbolise Clarissa's rigidity and desire to avoid emotional vulnerability.[8] This causes Clarissa to choose the more conventional, secure and safe Richard Dalloway. Richard "liked continuity; and the sense of handing on the traditions of the past." Like Clarissa, Richard finds comfort in traditional symbols such as Buckingham Palace. His identity is attached to these symbols which provide comfort. As a politician, Richard helps Clarissa fulfil her reputation. However, they lack complete connection as Clarissa's insecurity keeps her fearful of being sincere. Clarissa's attempts to be adored as the perfect hostess have dictated her interactions and relationships with others.[9]	7. This paragraph deals more directly with the consequences of Clarissa's façade and obsession with her reputation. 8. Peter is a connection to Clarissa's past. His judgement shows the hollowness of Clarissa's pursuit of the perfect hostess. 9. This part uses Clarissa's insecurity and desire to be admired to explain her choice long ago to marry Richard instead of Peter. This is a nice link to the thesis as it unites the past and present with Clarissa's deep-seated desires for status.

PARAGRAPH 3

The stream of consciousness style Woolf employs enables the reader to delve into Clarissa's vanity and ambitions.[10] Whilst Clarissa is presently occupied with maintaining her status as the perfect hostess, her ambitions extend beyond this. Clarissa truly desires adoration and influence, with hosting parties a mechanism to reaching this goal.[11] Clarissa's introspection and flashbacks to Bourton present her current despair and yearning for the simplicity and pleasures of the past. Clarissa compares herself to Millicent Bruton who has a similar reputation for her lunch parties. Through Lady Bruton, Clarissa saw "the dwindling of life; how year by year her share was sliced." The metaphor represents Lady Bruton's age and the effects it has on her appearance. This highlights the inevitability of age and its power to hinder one's dreams. Clarissa's spirit is eroding, undermining her chance to be truly fulfilled. Clarissa's duties as a hostess give her the opportunity for excitement in an otherwise insipid life. Her parties help to satisfy her desire for purpose and provide a reason to endure the pain of her illness. Clarissa rejoices in the belief that her parties are in service of others. She views them as unifying and a gift, "an offering; to combine, to create; but to whom?" The rhetorical question reveals that despite Clarissa's best efforts to forge a fulfilling life, insecurity remains deeply embedded within her. This is manifested "in the depths of her heart an awful fear" of being alone, unwanted and forgotten which Clarissa must grapple with. At the end of the novel, Woolf reveals how Clarissa is determined to pursue her passions more authentically and decisively than remaining transfixed as the perfect hostess.[12]

10. Dealing with structural features like stream of consciousness is a good way of exploring Woolf's purpose behind Clarissa's portrayal.

11. This part counters the statement in the question, furthering the argument that Clarissa's role as a hostess is a way of fulfilling her more base goal of being venerated.

12. The comparison to Lady Bruton reflects Clarissa's underlying fear. This establishes Clarissa's intentions with her parties as a way of coping with insecurity and a sense of inadequacy.

CONCLUSION Clarissa's youthful ambitions conflict with her present obsession with status. Her parties enable Clarissa to present herself as a respectable and valued member of the upper class. Peter sees through Clarissa's façade and her internal struggle with insecurity shows she is unfulfilled. Her pursuit to become the perfect hostess is emblematic of her desire to be adored and venerated but does not define her entire life. Clarissa's passions are reinvigorated as she confronts her mortality.[13]	13. The conclusion summarises the essay's central argument and connects with the final scene of the novel.

Essay Three

QUESTION: Virginia Woolf's *Mrs Dalloway* is about the control society has over the individual. Discuss.

ESSAY	COMMENTS
INTRODUCTION Virginia Woolf's *Mrs Dalloway* presents societal control as powerful and destructive but not absolute.[1] Individuals have the freedom to choose whether they give in to society's rigid expectations or fight ardently for personal liberation. Traditional institutions are heavily controlled by aristocrats who seek to preserve power at the expense of others. This suppresses individuality and sincerity, and forces individuals to decide how they respond to a repressive society where they have little influence beyond their own actions.[2] **PARAGRAPH 1** The powerful elites oppress the freedom of others and are desperate to maintain their authority and control. The post-war period saw society transform and a greater emphasis placed on individual freedom, especially through democracy, workers' rights, and feminism.[3] These developments threatened the aristocrats' grasp on power.	1. The thesis has some complexity to it which is important for a discuss question where we want to consider both sides. Here, we are saying that society has significant control over the individual but not total control. 2. The points of the essay are introduced concisely and relate directly to the thesis. 3. Important contextual information is given to explain the origins of the clash between aristocrats and the lower classes.

Sir William Bradshaw is a ruthless, uncompromising man who finds joy in the power he wields over his patients. Sir William enforces proportion by ostracising patients that do not reflect English values and order. Sir William "made England prosper, secluded her lunatics, forbade childbirth, penalised despair." This illuminates the cruelty of Sir William as he swiftly oppresses his patients. Sir William's methods of sending patients away to preserve social order represents the abuse and corruption of power and tendency of those with control to torment others. Septimus Warren Smith is one of Sir William's victims whose individuality is stripped and no hope for rehabilitation. Septimus finds himself "alone, exposed on this bleak eminence, stretched out". The metaphor highlights his vulnerability to the wrath of Sir William whose mission is to remove society's flaws from the public view.[4] Septimus is crushed by the weight of society's abandonment which leaves him fearful and numb. This prevents his capacity for intimacy and happiness. Septimus is driven to suicide to escape this overwhelming, oppressive force. Dr Holmes is another figure who upholds the power of traditions and institutions for personal benefit. He attempts to escape culpability for Septimus' suicide by feigning shock when talking with Mrs Filmer. Dr Holmes' rhetorical question, "Who could have foretold it?" accentuates his cruelty and apathy.[5] This thereby reinforces the powerful control society has and how the lack of support crushes an individual suffering mental illness.	4. Sir William's cruelty and obsession with proportion is analysed to showcase the power elites have over others, particularly vulnerable people like Septimus. 5. Dr Holmes' attempts to escape blame and responsibility are used to illustrate the power of institutions who face little consequences.

PARAGRAPH 2

Traditional institutions are historical sources of power and control. The maintenance of traditions discourages individuality and authenticity as growth and progress is seen as destructive. Generations are depicted as identical when conventions are observed. When there is no resistance to the control of society, generations "vanished, like leaves, to be trodden under." The simile conveys that individuals are isolated and vulnerable to the forces of society. Inaction only perpetuates suffering, inequality and conformity.[6] Aunt Helena epitomises the traditions of English society. She embodies the social norms which stifle freedom and individual control. This is evident as Aunt Helena admonishes Sally Seton's behaviour as disorderly and reckless.[7] Sally's fearless and wild youth has been abandoned as the "lustre had gone out of her." This symbolises how Sally's vitality has suffered due to her giving in to restrictive conventions. The unbridled thrill and energy of Sally's youth is undercut by her marriage to an uninspiring "bald man with a large buttonhole." The unflattering description depict Sally's conformity as a barrier to personal fulfilment.[8] Millicent Bruton is another character whose aspirations have suffered due to traditions that are taxing and difficult to penetrate.

6. The power of institutions is furthered here as extending beyond just one generation.
7. Aunt Helena is a symbol for tradition. Using Aunt Helena as evidence highlights the effects on individuals when they fight against tradition.
8. Sally's transition reflects the significant power of society to distort one's nature. Sally was very rebellious and wild, but has been tamed and is now well-adjusted to society.

Lady Bruton desires to use her intelligence and leadership as a general, but this dream is locked as she is "debarred by her sex." The patriarchal society typically excluded women from the public sphere and denied them equality and opportunity. This leaves Lady Bruton deeply dissatisfied and mournful of her position. Through Sally and Lady Bruton, Woolf interrogates the choking control society has over individuals who aspire greater freedom and autonomy.[9] **PARAGRAPH 3** Whilst society has enormous influence and control over individuals, it is not total. Individuals still retain free will, even in a world with limited options or little hope. It is the way that people respond to societal pressures that defines their character. Richard Dalloway finds it difficult to express his emotions and love for Clarissa. At times, their relationship is strained and distant. However, Richard's love remains and he is "eager, yes, very eager, to travel that spider's thread of attachment between himself and Clarissa." The spider's thread symbolises Richard's motivation to reinvigorate his relationship with Clarissa and build the courage express his love to her. Genuine human connection and love can be attained despite a repressive, controlling society.[10] Septimus felt trapped by society, particularly the oppressive Dr Holmes. His suicide was an expression of freedom, a rebellion against society by taking control in his final moments. Septimus' "Death was defiance. Death was an attempt to communicate" authentically and sincerely. The metaphor of death represents its power as Septimus dictates his destiny and escapes the tortuous pain at the hands of merciless institutions.[11]	9. Lady Bruton's suppression is due to the conflict between her dreams and a patriarchal society. This also highlights the extensive power of society and the impacts this has on personal satisfaction and fulfilment. 10. This paragraph takes the other perspective of the statement by arguing that ultimately individuals have control over their lives. A variety of characters are analysed to show how this can be seen in a range of circumstances and relationships. 11. Septimus, despite the overwhelming oppression he faced by institutions, still had enough control to decide how his life ends. This suggests individuals have greater power than society at determining their own fate.

Clarissa reflects on Septimus' act and questions, "had he plunged holding his treasure?" Treasure symbolises a person's spirit, the essence of their being. Clarissa contemplates whether Septimus maintained his spirit by exiting a repressive world on his own terms. Clarissa is detached from her past self as she leads a life of despair. Thus, Woolf showcases how, like Septimus, Clarissa now has the chance to seize control and revert to her base passions.[12] **CONCLUSION** Individuals must navigate a tumultuous society to find their identity and place in the world. Societal control is a powerful force that encourages conformity and hinders individuality. However, societal control is bound by the inherent freedom that all people have to respond to societal pressures, conventions and institutions. Individuals have agency to resist or succumb to the powerful forces of society.[13]	12. Clarissa's realisation of Septimus' individual power through his genuine act of communication inspires her. It is possible she may choose to pursue her passions and refuse to conform anymore to society's will. 13. The conclusion cements the essay's thesis and restates the main arguments presented. Note that different descriptions and phrases are used so that the essay does not feel repetitive.